KV-028-902

ADVANCED
GYMNASTICS FOR WOMEN

JUNE ALLISON

Advanced
Gymnastics for Women

STANLEY PAUL

UNIVERSITY OF GLOUCESTERSHIRE
Oxtalls Campus
Oxtalls Lane
Gloucester GL2 9HW

STANLEY PAUL & CO. LTD
178–202 Great Portland Street, London, W.1

AN IMPRINT OF THE   HUTCHINSON GROUP

London Melbourne Sydney
Auckland Bombay Toronto
Johannesburg New York

First published 1963

796.41

ALL

© June Allison 1963

*This book has been set in Baskerville type face. It has
been printed in Great Britain by The Anchor Press,
Ltd., in Tiptree, Essex, on Antique Wove paper.*

14,032

P. E.

Contents

Illustrations

Foreword

This book is intended to help the beginner, the advanced student and the coach alike. Much of the book deals with gymnastics from the coach's point of view, but it is hoped that it will satisfy the needs of a would-be gymnast who may not be fortunate enough to have a qualified coach.

It is a well-known fact that on the Continent gymnastics takes its rightful place among the great sports: indeed, it is recognized as one of the greatest. In Britain lack of finance and backing have tended to make it a 'hole-in-the-corner' sport, but now, thanks to television and publicity, we are at last being put on the sporting map. The constant work and dedication of a few strong-minded people in Britain is at last bearing fruit. Severely handicapped as we are by our home-made equipment, gymnastics is spreading very rapidly, so rapidly indeed that the need for qualified coaches is increasing with every day that passes.

In Britain we have no gymnastic coaching schools, therefore we have to rely upon knowledge gleaned from abroad, films and photographs. As a result, we are usually several paces behind the gymnasts with whom we compete. Experience gained in international matches is invaluable, but, alas, once more, such matches for us are few and far between. Our usual cry is 'lack of finance', but the cry cannot be heard too often, in the hope that one day we may be able to compete on equal terms with our Continental friends.

Lack of a school for coaches has put myself and other coaches in the unhappy position of having to solve gymnastic problems by the time-taking method of trial and error. How much easier would be our task if we had the 'know-how' at the start.

The material for this book has been collected at random over the four years that I have been training eighteen-year-old Monica Rutherford, the holder of the Women's Individual Gymnastic Championship of Great Britain, together with the other members of Fulwell Olympic Gymnastic Club. In these four years gymnastics in our club has developed from very meagre beginnings to a flourishing club in which eighty girls partake of this exciting sport each week.

I should like to thank most warmly all the coaches in Britain, both men and women, The Central Council of Physical Recreation and Sunderland Education Authority for their assistance along 'The Gymnastic Way'.

JUNE ALLISON

Introduction

Gone are the days (I hope for ever) when every child is expected to perform the same movement at the same time in the same way. Educational gymnastics has brought us this freedom, which must be exploited to the full. Perhaps it would be true to say that it has been exploited to the full and the hands of the clock turned back a little to a more sound foundation on which we can build advanced gymnastics. Educational gymnastics provides an excellent stepping-stone to higher things, but so many of our physical educationists these days (and here I mean P.E. teachers on the whole) have a knowledge of educational gymnastics and that alone. How many students in college could honestly explain what these types of movements are: tinska, straight-leg lever, hock half-turn, etc.? Yet if asked to explain a stroke in swimming or a bully in hockey they could do so extremely adequately. Perhaps in argument the reply would be that tinska, hock, etc., are only names given to movements and that terminology is not important. Yet these moves, though advanced ones admittedly, could be accepted into a wider range of movements and absorbed into the education gymnastics system if the students in colleges knew of their existence and were able to coach them.

How much more exciting for the children would be a term's work based on 'flight' if the teacher were able to coach individual movements such as handsprings, back-flips, etc., where this flight was needed. It is from such

themes that Olympic floor work develops. The gymnast
has at her disposal one and a half minutes and five seconds
for a finish. Into this time she must endeavour to include
rolls, springs, movements backwards, balances, leaps,
spins and turns, dancing steps of such a nature that they
provide links between the agilities and more static positions. Above all, the whole sequence must give variation
in speeds and strength of movement, must show mobility
and yet control, and should be performed with apparent
ease. How many of Laban's basic principles could be
interpreted into such a piece of work? How much more
pleasing, though, will such a piece of work be if included
in it are springs from hands, feet, head, leaps from feet
on to hands and springs backwards into the air to land on
feet.

Now it is significant that terminology must be applied
if the student is to be able to clarify her own ideas of what
may be included in such a wide term as 'springs'. Springing from the hands has obviously resulted in *handspring*
and similarly *headspring* and *neckspring*. Springing from
the feet on to the hands has resulted in a series of vaults
simply because an obstacle has been placed in the way.
Of necessity, vaults have been named, though basically
they are 'How can you get over the box using hands
only?' It seems rather pointless to avoid the name of a
specific vault—we don't evade the issue when it comes to
arithmetic, which is, after all, only mental gymnastics!

In the following chapters I have set out agilities,
dancing steps (artistic gymnastics), preparation on beam
and bars, together with many advanced moves at championship level, in an endeavour to show how I am correlat-
ing advanced gymnastics into my school curriculum
without taking away the freedom of the individual in
choice of work and themes.

I

Agility

Agility is the commonly recognized term given to a group of movements which fall into a definite pattern as opposed to the freer type of dance movements used in advanced floor work, though both require nimbleness and an agile body and brain. By this we mean the kind of work usually performed on mats at the beginning and progressed to the floor as advancement in technique becomes more apparent—for example, a handspring or a fly spring. Each individual will perform such a movement in his or her own way, thereby allowing for individual style, but, nevertheless, certain coaching points common to all must be adhered to if the finished movement is to be of any value. The gymnasts will approach the movements in different ways, will develop different faults and will have, no doubt, different degrees of success. It is from the recognition of this there springs the major difference between coaching and teaching. A coach must be able to recognize the most important faults in a gymnast's action and be able to correct them before a bad movement habit has arisen, Let us take, for example, the handspring. When teaching the handspring it is of little consequence whether the gymnasts land in a crouching position or in a high position, but as the ultimate aim is to land in preparation for another movement, the coach must step in to see what is the cause of the low position—probably bent arms.

Throughout this chapter I intend to single out movements giving common faults and corrections and to suggest as many different ways in which a movement can be approached and terminated.

For clarity the chapter has been divided up into:

(a) Agility which does not demand spring.

(b) Agility which requires specific loosening exercises of the average gymnast, e.g. body bends and splits.

(c) Agility which requires both springs and the ability to 'hollow out in the air'.

(a) *Agility which does not demand spring*

Into this section come all the movements of a rolling, handstanding and cartwheeling nature, and some simple balances.

Rolls
All rolls have these two things in common: the rounding of the spine and the tucking in of the head.

Forward roll
This should be approached carefully with an absolute beginner to avoid the common fault of standing on the head instead of tucking it in.

COACHING: The knees should be bent into a crouch position, the hands placed on the mat in front of the feet, the head tucked in to the chest and the body allowed to roll over smoothly, each part of the spine touching the mat in turn. Come up to stand. The bent knees should be gradually straightened to produce a more streamlined effect. The ability to roll smoothly is recognized as a safety measure when falling forward or from a height. The roll can be developed so that the gymnast stands up, one foot in front of the other, thereby giving an easier follow-on to the next movement. Dive rolls will be dealt with in the section requiring spring.

Backward roll

There are many different ways in which the gymnast can learn to roll backwards. There is not a right and a wrong way but several different ways. If a definite pattern is required then the roll takes on a more formal shape.

COACHING. Similar to the forward roll, the backward roll can be approached by the suggestion of curling into a small ball and tumbling backwards. This in itself will produce several different positions of finish. The starting position may vary too, but as the legs lift over the head the aim should be to keep the legs straight and tensed at the knees. This once accomplished, the gymnast will have no difficulty in attempting rolls of a more definite nature. If a symmetrical roll is required then the weight must be put on to both hands at once and should pass over the top of the head—not by avoiding the head and turning it sideways.

Backward roll on to one knee

From sitting or standing, keep the legs straight and roll backward until legs are above the head. At this point 'split' the legs, placing one knee on the ground and the other leg high in the air. The head should be thrown back to develop a sense of line. This position can be followed by pushing the weight backwards on to the kneeling leg and actually sitting on the heel. The arms may take up positions most suitable to the individual.

Backward roll into straddle stand

Repeat the roll until the legs are above the head, then split both legs and, keeping them straight, place the feet sideways. The weight should then be transferred from the hands to the feet. The roll can be varied by altering the width of the space between the legs.

Backward roll on to one foot

The preliminary part of the roll remains the same, but a

little more lift is required to move the body weight from the hands, over the head on to the foot (one foot). The free leg may be lifted back to produce a balance standing position.

Backward roll to finish with body in a flat position (prone)
The same preparation is required as for the straddle, but in this case the legs remain together and press backwards along the mat. The body may be lifted up by the arms to develop a slight hollow.

Backward roll to handstand
This is a much more advanced movement, requiring timing and strength. The body weight is thrust upon the hands very quickly and at the same time the legs thrust backwards and upwards to reach the handstand position. The chin, which is resting on the chest in the roll, must be quickly lifted up so that the head is thrown back to maintain the handstand. The head must not be thrust sideways, otherwise the upward thrust of the body weight will be unequally distributed. This will result in an uneven push of the hands.

Rolls sideways
These kinds of rolls are often neglected and yet they can give a very pleasing 'link up' between other movements. They are the kinds of rolls that develop when 'playing' with a movement, e.g. kneel up on the left knee with the other leg out sideways and stretched. Roll across the shoulder to finish in starting position by placing the left arm under and across the body.

It is a common experience for children to roll down a slope while they keep 'like a log'.

This method of turning from back-lying to prone-lying can be a very useful way of regaining a standing position in readiness for another movement especially if, on the last turn, one knee bears some of the body weight.

Handstanding movements

Certain basic principles must be brought to bear if the gymnast is to learn a correct handstand, i.e. one from which other movements can develop as well as one that can be held indefinitely. These principles are: the position of the arms in relation to each other, the head poise and the complete extension throughout.

Handstanding is not a natural acitivity, therefore it demands constant practice to develop not only the body but to attune the delicate organ of balance which enables the gymnast to 'stand on her hands'.

COACHING: The hands should be placed on the floor shoulder width apart, the fingers slightly spread to give a greater base on which to balance. The head should be held back (i.e. a short neck at the back) and the whole body held in a state of tension or stretch. Special emphasis should be placed on the stretch of the legs and feet. This excessive stretch should never be relinquished in a handstand—once it is, the balance is lost and the feet return to the floor. Girls, on the whole, are inclined to hollow rather more than boys in a handstand, thereby holding the handstand by pure relation of one part of the body on another. The shoulder joint should be directly over the wrist and the feet directly over the head. Most handstands follow this pattern, but there are exceptions to the rule. A very stiff back or shoulder will result in the feet being farther over the head.

The handstand is one of the most important agilities because from this position we find numerous other agilities developed, such as the handspring, walkover, backward walkover, etc. It is also important because it gives such a wide variety of starts and finishes.

Some of these are dealt with now.

Kick to handstand and change legs

The handstand position is gained, but the legs never come

B

together. Instead, the first leg to be put into the air becomes the first leg down again. This results in the legs
changing places whilst the weight is on the hands. The
change of legs can be coached so that each leg shows a
'split' position forward and backwards. The body weight
remains poised above the wrists and the seat remains
above the shoulders.

Handstand roll

In this roll the handstand position must be held for a short
time with the legs together and a slight hollow in the back,
head thrown back. After the slight pause, the elbows gently
bend, the head tucks in and a roll from shoulder to seat
is accomplished. The standing position may be resumed
by keeping both feet together all the time, by placing one
foot in front of the other and by finishing in long sitting
position and from there a backward roll to stand.

Handstand to lower to one knee

Here the important thing is that the weight of the body is
kept over the arms as they bend gently to allow one knee
to be placed on the floor. The free leg should be kept as
high as possible because this will help to maintain the
handstand position.

Handstand to straddle down

The basic principles of a handstand must be applied very
carefully in this handstand—the weight of the body kept
over the shoulders as the legs begin to straddle down, the
seat comes farther forward over the head to counteract
the weight of the leg lever. The more mobile the gymnast,
the nearer the feet can be placed to the hands. The legs
should remain stretched, the toes too, until the very last
second before touching the ground. The gymnast should
endeavour to feel that she folds at the hips while the seat

remains still. This same feeling can be applied to a hand-stand lower to the ground where the legs remain together. A much stronger lever is required, together with shoulder and wrist strength, because the body weight is transferred much farther forward over the wrists.

These lever positions can, of course, be used as a means of achieving a handstand as well as lowering from a hand-stand.

Handstand to chest roll
Similar coaching points arise here as those for handstand lower to one knee, but both legs must be kept stretched and the handstand maintained with the lower part of the body. The movement arises at the shoulders so that they move forward over the hands as the arms bend gently. The chin goes very close to the floor, therefore the gymnast should lower to this position and not collapse.

From these handstanding movements many variations can be developed, especially in conjunction with the backward and forward rolls. Hence the beginning of an agility sequence.

Simple suggestions:

(a) Handstand roll, forward roll to finish in long sitting, backward roll to straddle, sit back, join legs and backward roll to one knee. Swing free leg round and stand.

(b) Handstand, change legs to balance stand, swing forward free leg and sit down into backward roll on to knees, forward roll to stand, handstand roll to stand.

Not much space has been devoted to these sequences because in girls' work the tendency is to link up agility movements with dancing-steps, spins and turns.

Another movement which demands a basic handstand is the cartwheel, which should be taught to both the right and left. The cartwheel is essentially a sideways movement and should be taught as such. Once a good cartwheel has been achieved then variations and individual pre-parations can be used.

The gymnast should stand feet apart, arms outstretched sideways, head well up.

ACTION: Lean away from the side on which the cart-wheel is to be performed, i.e. to the right for a left-handed cartwheel, lift the left leg sideways and stretched, then throw on to it so a pattern is formed: left foot, left hand, right hand, right foot. The second arm should be held back, elbow beside ear, to prevent it from swinging across the body instead of overhead.

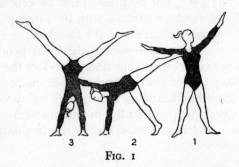

FIG. I

The practice of using a straight line on which to cart-wheel is an invaluable one. At all times the gymnast should think of stretching towards the ceiling with the toes extended, knees braced and the body in a stretched position. If the legs are kept straight throughout, then the legs will remain straight on landing.

Up to this point the stress has been on how a movement should be done. This to a modern educationalist may be astonishing, but the intention has been to give coaching on specific movements round which a freer type of movement can develop. I can hear 'Why should the legs be stretched in a handstand or a forward roll?' Why indeed? If curling movements are required, then the handstand roll must be adapted to suit. This applies to many movements, but there are some movements, which will be dealt with farther on, where bending of the legs prevents the actual aim from being achieved. Such is the handspring—the loss of whip in the legs by bending the knee or knees prevents the flight from developing successfully. But what variation can be produced on a handspring which has been coached correctly from the start? Such a variation is a handspring to land on the knees after first having passed through handstand at full stretch. The knees are quickly bent to land on them. This can be followed by a quick relaxation of the whole trunk, head on to knees, and if sequence work is required this position is ideal for symmetrical or asymmetrical development. The field for themes is greatly enlarged by the achievement of definite positions.

All the agilities explained up to this point have not required very much in the way of suppleness, so now the next section deals with movements requiring a much greater degree of mobility.

(b) *Agility which may require specific loosening exercises of the average gymnast, e.g. body bends and splits*

In gymnastics, the same as in other sports, some people have an ideal physique on which to work. A supple, lithe body makes gymnastics easier for the individual if allied with strength and co-ordination. A supple body can easily be strengthened but it is a greater problem to loosen a stiff body. Young children are ideal because they are generally supple and strength develops quite naturally as they practise the required movements, especially if they are able to follow a well-varied programme of activities. In most cases suppleness develops along the same lines, but occasionally the gymnast needs definite help in loosening up. This especially to achieve splits and backbends. Limbering and loosening is almost a book in itself, but some of these suggestions have proved to be of use:

Stiff shoulders

Handstand position with two helpers kneeling down. Helpers place one hand on the gymnast's hand, the other hand on the back of the shoulder. As the gymnast allows her body to fall over into a 'bridge', the helper exerts a little pressure on the shoulder in a backward direction.

Stiff back (and often mistaken for stiff shoulders)

(a) Back-lying, pushing into a bridge position, keeping arms straight and shoulders over hands. Rise on toes to give extra height. Partner may help to give extra lift.

(b) Prone-lying, arch back, attempting to touch head with feet; again gentle assistance may be given. No violent jerks should ever be used.

(c) Probably the most useful way is to practise the movement required. This usually proves to be the quickest and most satisfactory way, e.g. to achieve a handstand bridge to stand ('crab') practise the actual movement.

Body bends

One of the commonest of the body bends is the handstand crab or forward bend. In this movement it is essential that an extended handstand should be taught before the body is allowed to drop. If this is not coached right from the start then excessive hollowness will result, especially in a gymnast who is already supple. Such a crab throws too much strain on the abdominal muscles—not in the first part but in the endeavour to pull up to stand. The gymnast should place the feet on the floor rather than drop on to them. In this way a jerk is removed, especially if the standing position is attained by rising on the toes and using the knee extensor muscles. The crab or bridge will then be a much higher bridge position. Until a really controlled forward bend is achieved it is unwise to progress to walkovers and tinskas, which demand the body weight to be transferred on to one leg. Many children find one-leg movements easier because they can 'cheat' gymnastically by either leaving a hand behind on the floor or by pulling up unevenly. This procedure spoils the symmetry of a movement, but if the symmetric movement is thoroughly mastered first, then asymmetric ones can be developed very easily.

Asymmetric movements without spring

Forward walkover

In this movement the handstand position is passed through by one leg at a time. The leading leg in the preparatory position becomes the last leg on landing, the 'kick-up' leg being the leg on which to land. The body should be fully stretched throughout the movement, the head held back and a state of tension maintained in the limbs.

FIG. 2

This extension should be kept until the gymnast is upright again. A common fault is to land on a foot everted to great extent. This results in undue strain being thrown on the instep and it invariably means an uneven standing position due to the hands leaving the floor one at a time. Supple shoulders are as equally necessary as a supple spine in the performance of a good walkover.

Because forward movements can be reversed we come to the backbend walkover and the backward walkover, the difference between the two being that in the former the movement stops after the bend but in the latter it is one continuous movement. The backbend is a basic position for all backward hollow movements. Again extension is required upwards first, not backwards, as is commonly thought. The higher the reach upward before reaching backward, the safer the position will be. The arms and hands should reach above the head, then as the body goes backwards the head and arms should lead the way, the hands alighting on the mat in a controlled way, not with a bump. The position achieved is that of a crab. Now the gymnast must learn to thrust with one foot at a time to kick over, once again extending the body and legs in the air. The complete pattern is: standing weight on both feet, transfer weight to hands, now push the weight from one foot completely on to hands, then remove it to the standing foot.

Backward walkover

This is a progression on the backbend. In this movement the weight is over one foot only, the free foot pointing forwards. The arms are lifted and extended at the same time as the body. The weight remains over the standing foot until the hands reach the floor, but throughout the movement the free leg commences its arc from pointing in front to handstand position to standing position. Once this movement has been achieved, different finishing positions can be practised, but no matter which position follows, the head must be held back in order to see the floor for the placing of the hands. This backward walkover is symmetric with the arms and trunk but asymmetric with the legs.

Suggested finishing positions

1. Backbend walkover to arabesque.

2. Backbend walkover to handstand, lower legs together.

3. Backbend walkover to step back into splits.

4. Backbend walkover to splits position (front leg leading between hands).

5. Backbend walkover into handstand, chest roll.

6. Backbend walkover on to one knee (or two).

7. Backbend walkover into handstand and leg lever through arms.

These are just a few ideas on which many movements can be developed.

By being able to perform such a backbend movement the gymnast's scope for movement is widened considerably. Once safety in the movement is certain, then development can take place in altering the movement itself: e.g. walkover on to one hand and land on both feet; walkover backwards on to one hand at a time and one foot at a time; alter the basic position of the arms above the head but make sure that the body reach is kept; omit the extension of one leg during the movement and develop a leg pattern. Many are the ideas which can be built on one movement, especially with an imaginative gymnast.

Another movement which must be classed as asymmetric is the tinska. This movement, though not difficult, demands a degree of thought at first, especially with an older person. A youngster will try more readily without much thought and probably be most successful. This movement is a cartwheel position with the arms and upper trunk and a walkover with the lower limbs—almost two compelte agilities moulded together to form a pleasing movement. Asymmetric because the parts of the body do different tasks and yet symmetric in that the movement pattern is directly forward. The timing is that of a cartwheel, one, two, three, four, or hand, hand, foot, foot. The action should be thought of as a cartwheel, with the lower trunk turning rather more forwards than sideways.

Head positions can be varied—held back, turned sideways or backwards to look at the last foot to leave the floor. This alters the basic position slightly and leads to a more varied action. Once again, of course, with practice, this tinska can be done backwards too.

The backward and forward walkovers almost demand a split position in the air of the legs, and so this calls for the next movement which requires the extreme suppleness in the hip joints. Some people are fortunate in that they do not actually have to work very hard to achieve splits, but for those gymnasts who do not have this natural ability, there is nothing but continuous and regular practice, but splits should never be practised until the gymnast is warm or has warmed up.

Useful practices

1. Kneel on a cushion and slide the free leg forward, getting as near to the ground as possible. Work with both legs. This avoids unequal muscle development and stretch.

2. Support the body weight on two chairs by placing a hand on each. From this position bounce in splits. Change legs.

3. Partner help—arabesque position, gently push the extended leg higher.

4. Partner help—support the free or forward splits leg (back foot remains on the ground), gradually, with bounce, lower into full splits. Each individual will find the most useful way to attain her mobility.

In conclusion to these few words on movements requiring greater suppleness, I must add that they are simply a few selected because of their usefulness and are by no means the only ones of their kind. They are basic in that they appear in advanced floor work, but not in such a simple form. The approach to these movements can be varied, the movement itself changed and the method of 'arriving' altered so that what was at the beginning perhaps a backward-bend walkover scarcely resembles the finished movement. Here we have the use of a theme which will require variation in rhythm and speed. This is an isolated example to show how it has been used in a voluntary sequence, a backward tinska to alight, ready for a backward walkover to handstand (all performed slowly and deliberately); from the handstand the legs split very fast in the air to shoot the front leg between the hands into splits. The movement never stops. From splits the trunk rolls forward on to floor and a speedy spin is the method of recovery to the feet in preparation for the next movement.

Many of the basic agilities which have been discussed can be progressed by the introduction of spring or flight either before the movement or actually in it. This prompts the next major section on agility.

(c) *Agility which requires a spring*

Now the gymnast approaches the realm of more exciting agility because there is an element of courage required before launching herself into the air. Once again the gymnast may learn to spring forwards, sideways and backwards—the latter demanding much mental control as well as physical. Here also is the opportunity for creative themes based on work already understood. Flight is a common word in educational gymnastics, more especially thought of in terms of leaping into the air or leaping over obstacles, and it is, of course, apparent in any vault or jump. There is a wide field of parts of the body from which the gymnast may spring. This can be developed wonderfully if the ability to spring from most parts of the body is taught or coached. Springing from the feet is natural; springing from hands, head, knees, shoulders, etc., is far from an everyday occurrence, but it can be trained so that it becomes almost as easy to leap on to the hands as it is to spring into the air from foot to foot. What is it that enables a gymnast to elevate herself from feet to hands, etc.? It is the speed of the thrust and impetus gained, married together at the right time so that flight results. At first, in the learning stages, the elevation is not very great, but continued practice develops the muscles, gives strength and, above all, provides the co-ordination so necessary in the production of this spring. A degree of strength is very necessary in taking the weight on to parts of the body unused to weight-bearing, but the coach will have seen that all-round development of physique has progressed along with the basic training. Nothing is more infuriating that to wish to try a movement only to find that the limbs are not strong enough to control the weight. For simplicity this section has been subdivided into agilities which travel forwards and agilities which demand a backward spring.

Forward springs

The simple forward roll can develop into a most spectacular and a daring move requiring mental and physical skill in controlling the body weight forward and upwards in the air. This is the dive roll, which can be progressed to a hollow-back dive roll. The gymnast assumes a swallow-dive position in the air before tucking in the head and accepting the body weight on to the hands. This dive requires a very high degree of proficiency and the ability to time the movement to a split second. Certainly this is not a movement for a beginner gymnast even to anticipate. The flight or take-off is from two feet after a short but explosive run in which the forward speed is converted upwards. At the height of the movement the back is hollowed and the head thrown back; the arms may be thrown sideways. The thrust from the feet is so great that after the hollow position in the air the body reaches almost a handstand position. The arms should be brought forward quickly and only momentary weight taken on them before the head is tucked in to roll safely to stand. At no time should the arms be tensed on landing. The momentary support is rapid; only sufficient to time the tuck in of the head. This rather exciting forward spring is by no means the first spring that should be tried, but degrees of difficulty in spring rolls can be tried long before this flying-dive roll.

The most common of the early springs to be tackled is the handspring. Indeed, children use it among themselves as a measure of proficiency. A young gymnast experiences a handspring early and is excited by it, and from then on it becomes a measure or a rung in the ladder of gymnastic achievements. Usually the second rung in agility is claimed by a backflip and so on to somersaults (not to be confused with rolls).

The handspring is, once again, a basic move round which almost every one-footed spring develops. Many coaching points have been given for a handspring, but these three major ones have been found to be the most useful:

1. All points concerned with a handstand, i.e. straight arms, straight legs and head held back.
2. The hop in preparation for the spring.
3. The quick catch-up of the second leg.

The gymnast should practise the step-hop, the run, then step-hop and finally the run, hop and throw on to hands. This may be against a wall or against a partner's shoulders. The forward speed gained on the run has to be converted into upward power by the hop, then transferred into the 'handstand over' by the speed of the feet. At all times the arms should be straight and the head held back. The second leg or the thrust leg should catch up with the first leg in a handstand position. With beginners and in faulty handsprings the second leg is either just caught up before landing or doesn't catch up at all. This results in a fairly low position, which is probably twisted. One hand will most likely be left behind on the floor.

The aim in a high or hollow-back handspring is to stand erect in a ready position for another movement. At first individual style should be ignored until the movement is achieved, then development and individuality can be allowed to take over. I can hear a modern educational gymnast saying, 'Why shouldn't she leave a hand behind on the mat or why not individuality first?' Well—why not? There is nothing wrong educationally in performing a handspring asymmetrically provided that it can also be performed symmetrically. A bad movement habit such as this particular handspring is only bad in the sense that muscles are developed on one side only, and the poor landing position deprives the gymnast of progressing to a more advanced movement. This is taking only one bad movement habit, and making an issue out of it, to prove the necessity of foregoing the individual style until technique has been mastered.

Now back to the handspring. The feet should join together above the head—children can be told to think of midday on a clock and try to get the legs together before twelve or at twelve. A late catch-up will result in a forced high landing rather than a high landing due to the spring and speed necessary to make it so. A handspring done well is a joy to watch. The flight from the hands extends the body so that it is almost parallel with the ceiling before alighting lightly on the ground.

Once again it is easier to learn a handspring on to one leg, but once the catch-up leg has learned to delay in the air it is more difficult to teach the quick catch-up. From experience, coach the handspring to land on two feet first, then progress to land on one. The movement itself is very similar, but a greater degree of flight from the hands is required because of 'no catch-up', otherwise a fast walkover results. Once the movement is established, different arm positions can be adopted after the thrust. From the floor they can reach up above the head—they can remain behind the head, as in a very hollow back position, or they can be drawn in very close to the sides of the body, giving a 'limbless look'.

Once a really experienced handspring is achieved, landing positions can be used for experimentation. Already mentioned is the landing on one leg. This can be developed so that the free leg travels forward quickly into a splits position. Another idea, though rather advanced, is to give more speed and height in the spring, and instead of

FIG. 3

allowing the legs to relax when the feet touch the ground they are held in a state of tension so that the gymnast finishes in long sitting position with hands reaching towards the toes. The legs must be kept very straight and the toes stretched, otherwise the heels will bang on the floor. Another development is again a fast high spring, then, just as the feet get nearer to the floor, the knees are bent quickly, so that the gymnast arrives in a kneeling position. This is an ideal movement to develop for a theme on stretch and curl, because the terrific relaxation after the tension produces a curled position of the trunk on the bent knees.

All these progressions can be built only on a handspring which is technically correct and this technique can be achieved only by ironing out any movement faults which may develop as the agility is in the process of being mastered. In an ordinary handspring there is a moment of flight from feet to hands—the speed is needed instead, but if flight is introduced, so that the movement pattern is run, hop, flight, hands, flight, feet, then the agility has been altered slightly. This unusual placing of flight has resulted in the term 'flip handspring' or 'flip tinska'; yet another idea which can be exploited in the rather more

FIG. 4

static agilities, e.g. flip into a handstand; flip into a cartwheel.

From the handspring we move on to the tinska. The actual coaching and approach has been dealt with earlier, but the same thing applies to the flight here as in the 'flip handspring' except that the flight puts the weight on to one hand so that the pattern becomes run, flight, hand, hand, foot, foot.

An interesting theme could be developed here with older gymnasts to determine where flight can be achieved —at the beginning of a movement, at the end, in the middle or even once or twice in a movement. This could be carried on to all apparatus, but more especially on to the vaulting horse.

1 Part of a team floor exercise

2 Walkover

3   Handstand, drop over to splits. *N.B.* From off right hand

4   Splits position

No doubt this method of determining flight has been well tried before, but these more advanced movements lead to a greater field of knowledge, therefore a wider exploration.

The headspring is another forward-springing movement in which a little weight is borne on the forehead, though when the movement is fully co-ordinated it can be performed without any actual weight on the head. This action is derived from a two-footed take-off rather like that of a dive roll, indeed it very commonly follows a roll in a sequence. The body weight is pushed forward

Fig. 5

from the feet on to the hands and forehead momentarily, then the speed from the feet and the whip of the legs drives upwards lifting the weight from the hands again and so to stand. The angled headstand is a useful way of feeling the headspring position so long as it does not become the most important coaching point because this position is passed through, not held. After the spring from the feet to the hands and forehead the seat should over-balance a little in order to allow the hips to beat together with the whip from the legs. This whip should be upwards, not forwards. The extension of the body should result in the arms straightening and the hands being pulled away

C

from the floor rather than the head being pushed. The headspring is a movement often performed badly by girls because of the suppleness of the back. The back should be kept strong and the hips well flexed until the moment of flight from the head and hands.

A useful method of learning this movement is to execute it over a raised surface, perhaps a box top. This allows more time for the gymnast to feel the angled position before beating to stand.

In all springing movements it is wise to have a stand-in until the action is felt. There need be no feeling of inhibiting the movement or of taking away the freedom of the individual because many of these movements would never be tried if it were not for the confidence placed in the coach by the gymnast. I have said very little about standing by or standing in because the tendency in educational gymnastics is to allow the gymnast to do what she is able to do safely and without support. This is an ideal situation for some members of the class and many children will succeed, but they will not learn the more difficult movement simply by having a go. Some of the backward springs would never be attempted except perhaps by the daredevil in the class and yet there is no reason why many of the class should not become proficient in these advanced movements.

Gymnastics is gathering such a following and so rapidly that it is becoming increasingly important that the gym teacher should be able to coach more than educational gymnastics. During a teachers' training course comments such as these were heard on numerous occasions: 'All we learned to do at college was to relax and roll.' 'If only we had been able to learn to do and coach these movements too.' 'The girls at school saw a TV show and the next day they asked me to teach them a backflip. Of course, I hadn't a clue.'

On the Continent such a state of affairs does not exist.

All P.E. colleges and training colleges devote time to gymnastics because they realize that a well-trained gymnast can cope with almost any other branch of sport to a certain degree of proficiency. One of the Finnish gymnastic team wanted to come to England for three months to attend a P.E. college to gain a different outlook on Olympic gymnastics or advanced gymnastics. We had nothing to offer her!

However, in the north-east of England I can vouch for a nucleus of P.E. teachers who realize that modern educational gymnastics does not even start to touch the fringe of what can be done. It just doesn't go far enough. It gives a good basis from which to found gymnastics, but as to spending four, five or even more years on it alone—well, experience has shown this is where it falls down. In Britain we do seem to do things in a peculiar way; we swing over completely to a free type of gymnastics and yet we still build the majority of our gymnasia in Swedish style! Swedish equipment is in itself limiting. Now to get back to advanced gymnastics and forward springs.

Free walkover

This is the name given to a movement which is rather like a forward somersault from one foot, to land on one foot, but in a hollow position as opposed to the tuck in a forward somersault. These coaching points which I am going to give are based purely on experiment, i.e. the method by which Monica Rutherford learned to do a free walkover. First of all the gymnast must be strong enough to land on one leg (kept straight), otherwise sinking at the hips will result.

1. A short approach run only with a definite hop, as in the one-legged handspring, is needed (more run tends to make the move travel).

2. On the hop the arms should be up and forward;

extended from here they pull in very quickly so that the elbows point backwards. This starts the roll of the body.

3. The head should not be drawn into the chest, otherwise the forward rotation is too great.

4. The speed for the take-off should drive upwards whilst the arm action propels the body over the top. (By this I mean that the gymnast should imagine that there is a pivoting point in the shoulders round which the trunk and limbs rotate.)

5. To stand in for the movement is very necessary because the first feeling is to throw towards the floor. Two people may give a little shoulder lift to enable the gymnast to feel the turnover. Once the arm action is perfected in conjunction with the footspring it is better to delay supporting until the initial movement is made, i.e. support across the back once the forward somersault part has been achieved.

No doubt there is much in this coaching that a Continental coach would not approve of, but when trial and error are the only means at our disposal then we have no other choice.

I cannot stress too much, though, that this is an upward action which should allow an easy landing. Aim to be able to walk forward after landing without a break from the movement.

Forward somersault

Both the forward and back somersaults are simply curled-up rolls done in the air rather than on the ground. A trampoline can give a very good idea and feeling of tucking up in the air, but, of course, the spring from the trampoline is far greater than natural spring.

It can be a useful practice to learn a somersault from a take-off on a springboard so long as the action goes upward and not forward. Again a short run is all that is needed. A run, double take-off from the board, then spring upwards into the air, bringing the knees up to the chin. Progress further by raising the arms to bring them down strongly to the knees which have been pulled up. Care should be taken here not to hold too violent an arm action, otherwise the somersault may result by accident.

Once sufficient height has been achieved, the complete somersault may be tried. One or two people to stand in, or the use of an agility belt, is advocated. The action should be: run, spring up, then at the height of the spring whip the arms down to the knees and turn over. Open out just before landing. Unfolding too early will result in a semi-hollow somersault from which it is difficult to land. The stand-by should ensure that the gymnast turns over by supporting across the shoulders. In this way the forward rotation can be ensured.

When the somersault is in the early stages the tendency is to land with too much forward speed. This can be corrected by a slight 'push back' of the hips on take-off, to produce a landing rather more on the spot than forward.

The forward somersault does not seem to figure in women's work, either set or voluntary. Much more common is the back somersault.

Before any of the backward springs can be executed in sequence the gymnast needs to master the round-off or arab spring. This movement, on the whole, is not done well by girls in this country, the tendency being to whip the legs round the side instead of attaining a vertical position.

The round-off

This is a movement by which speed can be gathered on a forward run, then the body reversed so that a backward movement may follow. The take-off is primarily the same as for a handspring (i.e. the hop with arms raised), but the hands are placed on the mat one after the other as in a cartwheel. The shoulders should remain forward until the first hand is down. At the same time the whip from the leg (as in the handspring) speeds the body through a handstand sideways. Now the hips turn a quarter and at the same time the legs, which are together, are brought down to the ground rapidly. The movement should be practised slowly to ensure correct action, then speeded up. The feet must land on a straight line with the hands, otherwise when the backflip is joined to the round-off the throw will not be straight. When the speed is increased it helps to make the gymnast reach forward a little with the arms at the beginning of the round-off because it makes the hands leave the mat quickly in preparation for the next movement. A rebound should result from a good round-off; the feet should be together and pointing straight forward.

It is a good plan to be learning a standing backflip at the same time as the arab spring or round-off. In this way the link-up of the two movements will not take so long.

The standing backflip

This should present no fear or difficulties with young gymnasts who have been taught to do backbends and walkovers, because adding a spring to a movement is only a progression.

Stand-ins for support are absolutely essential when doing the actual flip, but there are two or three progressions which can be used.

1. Stand both feet together, reach up and back on to two hands, bring both legs over together and stand. Repeat this many times, gradually getting a little faster. Note—arms lead the way, head seeing the way!

2. The practice spring—stand both feet together. Bend the knees, allowing the weight to fall on the heels; jump upwards—not too vigorously at first because the tendency is to fall back. The drive should pass from the heels through the knees, but the body should not bend forward.

Now progress so that the arm action is included. The arms raised forward at shoulder level are lowered to the sides when the 'sit' or knees-bend is executed. From these drive upwards and backwards at the end of the thrust or drive from the feet.

A stand-in can ensure safety by timing this jump and placing a hand behind the head to prevent overbalancing during the jump.

The arm and leg action must be well co-ordinated to produce a good backflip. If the arms throw too soon the flip will be too high. If the feet do not thrust sufficiently there will not be a sufficient height to ensure space for the hands to land on the mat. The arms should be kept straight—the hands push off very quickly so that hand-stand position is achieved on the way through the back-flip. Most girls prefer to learn the backflip with two supports until the movement is correct, then to progress to the safety-belt.

The supports should kneel one on either side of the gymnast and place one hand on the back of the thigh, the other either across the small of the back or actually holding on to the waist. Young children are inclined to use their suppleness of back to attain a backflip instead of using thrust and arm action, although this usually disappears when the gymnast becomes stronger. It is a compensatory factor for lack of strength.

A row of backflips is a pleasing thing to see and to get this the flips must be controlled and speedy. One very high one promptly looses the speed and the succession stops.

To join together the arab spring and the backflip a useful method is for the gymnast to take two steps, turn backwards on the third, bringing the feet together, and do a standing backflip. This can be speeded up so that it almost resembles the finished thing.

If the foot-thrust is weak a useful method of coaching is

to do a backflip from a forward roll, i.e. forward roll to stand, thrust, backflip. The body position is such that the drive results from the heels.

The arab spring backflip should be taken in a safety-belt which will not slip. The supporting straps must be crossed to allow for going through round-off. The arab-spring backflip should be done slowly at first to check whether the feet arrive in line with the hands, then with two or three controlled steps the whole action may be performed with the supports bearing the whole weight of the body by the belt until the first backflip is over. The first one usually feels funny, but after that progress can be made quite rapidly. The round-off should be good, and the backflip good, before putting the two together. Confidence can be undermined by trying to forge ahead too quickly. Develop style and technique and the difficulty on high tariff movements will come with practice, the results being ultimately better because style will be there too.

And so to the back somersault.

Back somersault
This is in effect a backward roll in the air. These are much more commonly known and seen done from a standing position than the forward somersault. It is essential to get the feeling of tucking in in the air, and again a trampo-line can help, but the same feeling can be taught by using two supports to take the gymnast over.

The gymnast should jump upwards into the air, thrust-ing from the feet and ankles, not by bending the knees, to get height. The push is derived from the balls of the feet as opposed to the heels in the backflip. The arms should be thrown upwards, the body straight and head in line (not thrown back). When the utmost height has been reached the knees are brought up to the chin and the body thrown over. This is easier than a forward somersault because the gymnast can sight the floor sooner for landing. The tuck position is followed by an opening out to allow a good landing. A back somersault should be treated as quite a different movement from the backflip and it should not develop into a high backflip as is often the case. In any somersault the aim should be height first before turning over, not turning on take-off.

Having mastered the round-off the backflip can be brought into action again for the back somersault. The approach is the same, but more vigour is needed to drive upwards. The bounce from the hands to feet should be very determined and the legs kept very straight to ensure the bounce from the balls of the feet and ankles straight up in the air. There should be no falling backwards as in the flip. The round-off can be practised with a tuck jump at the end to determine whether there is any falling back. The knees should be brought up to the chin so that the body is closed. Now the complete movement can be developed either in a belt or with supports. Note especially that the arms must throw upwards for the somersault, not backwards as in the flip.

More advanced still is the round-off backflip back somersault. Each of these moves must be accurate in itself, then co-ordination will result with practice.

To develop a hollow-back somersault more height is necessary from the round-off. The legs must be kept even straighter and the drive upwards from balls of the feet and ankles more determined than ever. When the full height has been reached the head is put back, not jerked, and the back hollowed. The arms throw upwards into the air, but after turning over they should be brought in to the sides. If the hollow somersault is inclined to travel, the hips should be thrown forward slightly. This will bring it closer to take-off, though if the take-off and height are correct this should not be needed.

A pleasing combination is round-off backflip, backflip

hollow-back somersault, which when perfect can be developed to land on one leg, the other producing a lunging pattern for a finish.

I have attempted to include ideas, recognized coaching points and trial-and-error methods into this chapter on agility, which has been divided up into three groups, namely: agility without spring, agility requiring a greater degree of suppleness and agility demanding spring. In the latter subdivision forward springs and backward springs have been used.

2

Floor Work

'Rhythm, grace of form and motion—these can be found in every art and craft—in painting, weaving, embroidery, architecture, in the human body and in all things living. All of these can have grace or can lack it. The absence of rhythm, harmony and good form is associated with evil of thought, deed and character, whilst their presence, on the other hand, betokens moral excellence and wisdom.'

PLATO

Kinesiology? This is the science which investigates and analyses human motion or movement. Now, what is movement? Some extraordinarily clever word-phrasing by Plato has been used to try to prove that in reality there is no such thing as movement. Take, for example, an arrow shot from a bow. It has been written: 'A moving arrow either is where it is or is where it is not. If it is where it is, then it cannot be moving, since, if it were, it would not be there, and it cannot be where it is not.'

However, the purpose of this chapter is not to prove that movement is negative, interesting a piece of logic though it is, but to correlate the work in the previous chapters with the freer type of dance movements required to link up or to provide acceleration for the agility movements.

Floor work
This title embraces such a wide field in advanced gymnastics that it is necessary to define exactly what it comprises. In the true sense it differs from other branches

43

of gymnastics in that no piece of portable or fixed apparatus is required. Floor work includes the rather more formal agility, which has been under discussion in the previous chapter, and the freer type of movement, which is dance-like in its quality. It is with the latter that we are really concerned in this chapter.

On the Continent floor work is aptly named artistic gymnastics because of the high aesthetic qualities woven into the fabric of rather ordinary dancing steps and spins. The elevation provided by the ballet technique is much sought after, and many gymnasts are proficient in ballet as applied to gymnastics. On the whole, ballet tends to be too technically correct, i.e. the placing of the feet, but the poise, balance, carriage and confidence gained by ballet lessons is of great value. It is in the training of floor work of this nature that modern educational dance comes into its own. Dance provides the freedom, the opportunity for relaxation, followed by tension, the chance to develop flow and, above all, to express the inner feeling for movement whether it be a slow, sustained movement or a quick, light effort. It is in this that I feel lies the great difference between ballet and modern dance—ballet is stylized, modern dance is freer.

Yet we use many steps, leaps and spins and teach them bearing in mind the ballet technique, but with the freer feeling of modern dance superimposed.

Many gymnasts I know will not agree with this idea. On several occasions a piece of floor work has been executed correctly balletically yet it has lacked the sense of feeling which should make the piece a joy to watch.

In coaching floor work I have found modern dance training invaluable, i.e. in the formation of a piece of floor work—the knowledge of speed variety, flow, strength and space determination has offered much in producing a rhythmic sequence so effortlessly natural. I hope that this will help teachers who teach modern dance to link up their gymnastic work occasionally and attempt to produce a simple piece of floor work on the same style as that performed in Olympic Games and competitions of all kinds. The wide selection of music at our disposal enables a gymnast to choose something which is in keeping with her type of work and feeling for movement. Ingrid Föst, of Eastern Germany, is extremely fond of, and good at, executing very fast spins and butterfly leaps and so her music allows for this flair. Polina Astakova follows the rather more convential style of ballet pose and so works to recognized ballet music, whilst Eva Bosakova experiments successfully with rather more jazzy music which allows full scope for her Slav temperament, although it is carried out with Latin American dash.

Perhaps the secret in the success of the combination of music and gymnastics lies in the fact that a top-line gymnast has her own pianist who composes or plays for her instead of the gymnast endeavouring to work to a piece of music already set.

But enough about those gymnasts and coaches who are already at the top. We in Britain must try to copy them and develop a style of our own. We must practise the simple things before we can hope to do the advanced work we see abroad.

Because floor work is so much an individual thing it is impossible to put down in writing what the gymnast should do and what she should not do. It is essential, though, that she should know the basic steps used in ballet; be able to feel a movement from inside; and, above all, to be able to fuse the actual agility movements with the dance sequences so that the two together become one.

Almost any dancing, skipping or running steps can be used to produce acceleration before an agility. Within this lies the possibility of varying the speed of the steps to give added interest. A piece of floor work executed at the same speed and with the same rhythm has little to offer.

Aesthetically it becomes monotonous and something is required to wake it up. This something can be provided by the music, which will, in its turn, stimulate the gymnast, or if the music does not provide it then the gymnast must arrange her work so that the speed is varied to give liveliness to it. Because of the nature of the floor area, twelve metres square, turns play an important part in the make-up of the exercise. Listed below are some of the useful steps and spins which may be woven into floor work.

(a) Springs from one foot to the other.

(b) Springs from one foot on to two.

(c) Hops.

These are very energetic steps which cannot be repeated endlessly, so we come to travelling steps of lesser effort.

(d) Travelling steps and turning steps.

(e) Pirouettes—any kind of spin or turn comes into this section.

(a) *Springs from one foot to the other*

These are movements which determine elevation. In artistic gymnastics a great deal of elevation is required, so it must be taught. Natural spring is indeed a great gift, but much can be done to improve spring. To begin, use free running, gradually increasing the springing action from the ball of the foot. Push up from one foot on to the other so that the running becomes small leaps. This may be taught also, leaving the leg and foot behind to start the development of a 'split' jump in the air. Another useful elevation practice is to stand feet astride, thrusting the weight from one foot to the other sideways, then forward and backwards, aiming to stay poised above the floor as long as possible. This is strenuous when done properly, so the number of *jetés* should be limited at first. A *jeté* is any jump from one foot on to the other and it includes leaps in the recognized form. If the elevation required takes the form of a leap forward and upward the best method of increasing it is to practise the actual leap. This can be taken by leaping over small obstacles or covering distance by using chalked lines. The leap requires a strong thrust from the grounded leg—the thrust should pass through the ball of the foot and so raise the body from the ground. The free leg should reach up and forward, as though stepping over a high wall with speed. The leg pattern depends upon what is wanted—splits in the air, a stay position in which the front straight leg is bent up

FIG. 6

to an angle of 45 degrees then extended again to land, or a split change legs. In this the front leg swiftly changes to become the rear leg.

A *jeté* turn is a scissor movement of the legs when the first leg to be 'thrown' crosses the body. This initiates the turn. While the first leg is free, the second leg is thrown to take its place; landing is on the first thrown leg. It may be done like this: Step to the left on the left foot, throw the right leg extended across the body to the left. Quickly make the right leg take the place of the left and land on the left. This is known as a grand *jeté*. Often it is preceded by a step, close, step (*chassé*) to give more speed and impetus for the big leap. The *chassé* step may travel

sideways, forwards or backwards. A scissor-kicking movement, where one leg is thrown up after the other, may
be taken forward, but it may also be taken backwards.
Because of the nature of the hip joint, the back kicks do not
go nearly so high. So much for the legs, which provide the
motor power for the body, but the body must help to
maintain the elevation once gained and assist in turning
actions. Just as the legs may be placed forward, backwards
and sideways, so may the arms. Arm positions for leaping
movements provide interesting frames for the body provided that they are placed correctly. At all times there
should be a feeling of tension between the shoulder-
blades to give the right attitude to the shoulder girdle.
The shoulder girdle should not rise when the arms rise
or a hunched-up position will result. The arms may be
placed rounded above the head; one arm rounded above
the head, the other free to the side; both arms extended
upwards, sideways, obliquely, backwards; arms forward
and back in opposition to the leg or both arms carried
forward in front of the body at shoulder level. Some
positions will suit the gymnast more than others, and so
for voluntary work the most pleasing ones should be
selected. None of these arm movements will look correct
and pleasing unless the head position is good, i.e. in good
poise: the feeling when leaping should make 'everything'
go up to the ceiling—head, lifted trunk and limbs. A
droopy head spoils the effect at once. Leaping should make
the gymnast feel exhilarated. If she does it will show in
her work.

(b) *Springs from one foot on to two feet and vice versa*
These are not nearly so common in floor work because they
produce a stop. Usually the spring is rather cat-like,
especially when done sideways. This movement is called
assemblée because the legs join together before landing.
(This is used by a gymnast when vaulting and when using

Free leaping position

6　Free walkover

7 Flying dive roll

8 Landing from the roll

a run followed by a two-foot take-off for an agility.) Direction and speed may be varied.

The scissor is a jump from two feet together to land on one. This kind of movement is used a great deal on the beam.

FIG. 7

(c) *Hops*

This step does not figure very much in floor work either, when a true hop is meant, i.e. from one foot on to the same foot. But in 1960 the World Games set work provided it: 'Spring on to the left foot and hop three times in a small circle.'

(d) *Travelling steps*

These are more of a gliding nature, which provide direct link-up between agilities and produce the necessary acceleration. Running steps and step-hops often figure in an approach to agility too. These steps include: *Chassé* steps, i.e. step with one foot, close up the feet, step forward again with the first—step left, close right, step left. Travelling *pas de bas*—in this step the left foot is placed obliquely forward with the weight on it. The right foot is brought to the left, but then it glides obliquely forward to the right. The left foot is then brought up behind the right into third position. The step is repeated stepping to the right first. The travelling *pas de bas* may be done in a

D

gliding fashion, with the emphasis on the sideways movement, or it may be more springy and directed forward.
Arm pattern may be used to give added interest.

Often in floor work a gymnast thinks that she must use
many running steps to gain speed. With little practice
this can be improved upon by shortening the run but
making it more spirited. The effort here takes the place
of the distance.

A step, close, step, hop is used, with variation, very often
before a handspring or a round-off. It is useful to be able
to execute a handspring with such an approach for
team floor exercises. In this the gymnasts work as a team
for five minutes, showing all the similar requirements for
individual floor work but doing them together.

(e) *Pirouettes*

Many spins are used in floor work to alter path direction
primarily, but also to give added interest, e.g. instead of
running into a tinska the gymnast may spin once or even
twice before the tinska.

All turns are based on the circle of 360 degrees and so a
full turn signifies a turn through 360 degrees. Similarly a
quarter-turn 90 degrees, half-turn 180 degrees and so on.
For ease of interpretation the body should be regarded
when considering the turn, i.e. in a 360-degree turn the
body turnscompletely round, but the free leg may complete
only part of the turn. This is determined by what is
required. A full example is, with the left leg placed sideways, spin the 360 degrees to the right on the right leg.
The free leg may complete the spin, stop short 90 degrees
or go on 90 degrees, but the turn is still a turn of 360
degrees.

In all spins the body weight must be kept over the
standing foot. The spin should be on the ball of the foot
and the 'stop' of the spin controlled by placing the heel
down. A preparation of the arms is necessary to develop

a good spin and these can be varied according to the spin.

Forward spin. Weight on the right foot, the free leg travels in a clockwise direction, as does the body. The free leg may be bent or stretched or commence straight, bend, then stretch again. The starting position may be from feet astride or one foot placed forward. In this case the weight is transferred to the forward foot when turning to the right.

Backward spin. Weight on the right foot in this spin; the turn is in an anti-clockwise direction. The feet are placed one in front of the other and the weight transferred to the front foot. The left leg then travels in an anti-clockwise direction. The spin should be executed on the ball of the foot by pulling up to that position from standing with heels down. Usually the free leg is bent at the knee to give a quicker turn. This back spin is often used in a sequence, e.g. step forward left foot, right foot and spin backwards on the right repeat, left, right, back spin. The arms may be carried at shoulder height in a rounded position in front of the body. Equally pleasing is a position which spirals above the head on the turn (right arm spirals, left arm is carried free to the side on the turn, then the left arm passes across the front of the body).

Included in spins is the spinning jump, commonly called a *pirouette*. In this the spring is from two feet on to two feet, but the spring demands a turn also. The feet commence in the third position and finish in the same. The body must be kept very erect, otherwise the turning jump falls forward or sideways. Once again arm positions may vary according to what is required.

Once the gymnast is conversant with spins, leaps and turns she can link them together to form sequences. These will provide the necessary control because the second spin will not be successful unless the first is in balance. Here an intelligent versatile gymnast comes into her own because she can experiment with turns and movements, developing them as she goes along into final sequences for use in her floor exercise.

Now, the floor work so far has been on what the legs do. Equally important is the poise and carriage of the trunk and head. Without this polish the jumps look undignified and often clown-like. There must be a feeling of erectness in the spine just as in the work on the beam, but the trunk, head and limbs must all work together as one to produce movement throughout the body. The head plays an important part in controlling spins (the quick flick round of the head when successive spins are being used) and it is the first part of the body which can set the tone of the movement. A drooping head spoils any movement even when the trunk and limbs perform faultlessly.

The trunk often acts as a less mobile part of the body to give direct contrast to the arm and leg movements, but more often the feeling is transmitted from the centre of the body in a wave-like motion to the limbs, hands and head. It is this inner feeling which emanates throughout the body which makes a dancer or a gymnast able to perform with just something more than technical correctness.

Very often in floor work we talk about a movement followed by a poise. A poise differs from a balance in that the balance is actualy held whereas the poise is almost a recovery, e.g. a held position for a split second, a hover on one foot or a momentary state of tension. These poises add interest to the work because they can take so many different forms. There is not time enough or space enough to describe all of these but a few are listed.

1. Poise on one knee, arm extended above the head.
2. Poise on both feet, arms outstretched.
3. Poise leaning backwards into a lunge.
4. Hover on one foot, arm pattern showed.
5. Hover on both feet, arms upstretched.
6. Hover on one foot, free leg bent at knee, arms obliquely backwards.

FIG. 8

FIG. 9

FIG. 10

It should be borne in mind that all these poise positions can be 'played with' to find more pleasing lines and arm pattern.

Actual balances are not used so much in women's work as in men's, but arabesques appear occasionally in set work. If a balance is used then it must be shown as an actual stop, since wavering balance creates a poor impression.

The arabesque as shown in Fig. 11 gives a pleasing line and the recovery from it produces a contrast, i.e. the straightness of the arabesque followed by the supple

FIG. 11

movement of legs and trunk. Similarly, as on beam, a balance can take many forms. The arms may be both extended obliquely backwards, the trunk arched to give a high line. The arms may extend forward to touch the ground, the legs keeping the line obliquely by being raised as high as splits position. Arabesques depend a great deal on the mobility of the gymnast. If a split position of the legs is not possible, then the arabesque itself must be altered to suit the mobility of the gymnast. (See section on balances in Chapter 3.)

So far the floor work has entailed only standing positions. The gymnast must, as on the beam, incorporate standing, sitting, kneeling and lying positions, but they are

passed through, not held. Fig. 8 gives a suggestion of standing up from a kneeling position using, first, trunk extension
sideways, trunk flexion in order to rise, then trunk extension again into a poise. The No. 1 movement in Fig. 8
can be arrived at from a spin. It can be altered to sit on
one heel instead of kneeling (World Games floor work)
from a spring upwards.

Back- and front-lying positions arise frequently from
splits position. Front-lying as shown in Fig. 12.

This movement can be continued by extending the
arms to arch the back and squatting the feet between
the hands to sit. From splits, also, the gymnast can roll

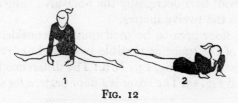

1   2

FIG. 12

forward on to the diaphragm (keeping back arched) to
take the weight off the hips; quickly bend one leg and
stand. In this way splits, a turn and standing position are
joined together. To achieve back-lying from splits, the rear
leg must swing round to join the front leg and at the same
time she should roll backwards on to the shoulders. A
standing position may be attained by continuing into a roll
or rolling back from the shoulders and up to stand, passing
through a 'V' sit position with the legs. Very speedy
rolling movements are extremely popular because they
provide direct contrast with the extended legs and springing movements from the hands. Very often these speedy
rolls are spun into—the gymnast scarcely touching the
floor. Many of the agility movements taken in the previous
chapter will put the gymnast in a position from which she
can work out her own methods of continuing, standing or

rolling. It is virtually impossible to cover anything like the ground in such a short chapter on floor work, but if these following notes are used to develop ideas on floor work then the coach will be able to produce a first piece of work on which she can progress herself. These suggestions are some of the methods employed when working out floor-work exercises for Monica Rutherford.

Composition of floor work

Floor area twelve metres square—this is a very good area on which to work, but unfortunately it is larger than any of our standard gymnasia, which measure forty by seventy feet, the wall bars decreasing the floor area sufficiently to break into the twelve metres.

1. The floor area to be used must be considered—use as much of the space as possible by straight curving and oblique paths. (See Fig. 13.) N.B.: The difference between Fig. 14 and Fig. 13. The latter is a floor pattern for set work.

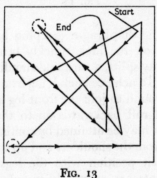

FIG. 13

2. Decide on the piece of music to be used, which must be between one minute and one minute and thirty seconds. Waltz tunes are very suitable for floor work, also 6/8 time, which adds more interest to the music.

3. Check carefully on the number of bars to be used, then break them up into smaller appropriate blocks, e.g. a

sixty-four-bar piece may be broken down into four blocks of sixteen bars.

4. Within the first block of sixteen bars decide what the starting movement will be and the same in the final sixteen bars for the finish. Then into each block of sixteen put in roughly the agility movements which will be included. They can be moved around at will if necessary in this way; the agility does not appear all at once, leaving the gymnast with nothing to do at the end except repeat movements. Round the agility movements the link-up acceleration and leaping movements can be added, depending on how they fit in with the agility.

5. Determine the floor pattern for voluntary work as the exercise progresses, but keeping in mind full coverage of the floor area. Spinning movements will fit in more easily at the corners when first starting to make up an exercise.

6. Take into consideration the placing of eye-catching movements. So often an eye-catching movement is used as a start and placed so that it comes almost at the edge of the area, causing the gymnast to hold back. Choose the most suitable place for a movement, not just at the beginning and the end.

7. Avoid movements of strain. Omit difficulty until it can be achieved with apparent ease.

8. When blending the movements together, consider not only the floor space but the space above the gymnast, e.g. a high leaping movement may be followed by a low rolling movement or a fast high springing movement followed by a low curling movement. Consider, also, speed variations. Avoid the same monotonous rhythm. If possible choose music with variations in speed or, better still, have it played so that it fits the gymnast's work. This is ideal, but of course it is more difficult to get the exact timing of one and a half minutes without many attempts.

9. Even though marks are allotted for difficulty and technical execution, general impression plays a very

great part. A well blended, controlled piece of work will merit more marks than a difficult piece with stumbles and falls, because style throughout should be the aim. If style is good difficulty will follow.

The World Games floor exercise follows, together with the floor pattern. This is a difficult piece of work to interpret because of the many spins. Take each block of bars separately (numbers on diagram 14 which compare with the numbers in the text) and work each block out. Don't attempt to look at it as a whole. If necessary, spend time on only two or three bars. Gradually it becomes easier to interpret set work when the terminology is familiar.

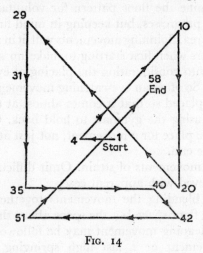

FIG. 14

WORLD GAMES 1962

SET WORK—WOMEN

(Prague)

Floor Exercises

The exercise begins in middle of area—music 3/4 time.

Contestants will be required to furnish their own music in 3/4 time.

1–2. From start position, raise arms sideward, body, arms and legs supple (3rd beat of 2nd measure).

3. Spring to left leg, bend body to right, raise right leg sideward and cross it before left leg, turning 90 degrees to left, place right foot, right arm forward, left arm to rear, take 2 steps forward, left, right, with 1/2 turn to left on right leg. lowering arms, knees supple.

4. Spring on right leg thrusting left leg stretched to rear, arms obliquely downward, left forward, right to rear, palms down, body extended.

5. One step with left foot, lowering arms, stride jump, right leg forward bringing arms up to horizontal, left forward, right to rear.

6. Lowering arms, one running step with left foot, thrust right leg forward, spring and 1/2 turn to left with scissor thrust of legs (turning jump), and land on right leg, left leg to rear, with simultaneous circling of arms from front to rear in sideward position.

7. 1/2 turn to left on right foot, 3 quick steps, left, right, left, lowering arms.

8. Lunge forward on right leg bent, deep body bend to rear, head turned left, raising arms forward, right arm rounded above head, left arm horizontal.

9. Shift body weight to left foot, 1–1/8 turn to left (405 degrees), on bent left leg, right leg raised sideward before bringing it forward at end of turn, bending body to right, head turned to right, arms sideward (right arm and right leg are parallel).

10. Lunge forward on bent right leg, lowering arms obliquely to rear and bringing them forward again, body inclined forward (45 degrees) with slight raise of left leg.

11. Shift weight on left leg, turn over to rear with thrust of right leg, then left leg to arrive at . . .

12–14. Balance standing on right leg with arms obliquely downward, right arm slightly more forward.

15. Straighten up and place left foot to rear, pivot on left toes 180 degrees to right, right leg bent with foot at level of left knee, arms rounded in front of body.

16. Place right foot on toes, bend left leg with left foot

behind right leg, turning 180 degrees to right on toes of right foot, opening arms.

17. Immediately place left foot behind right foot, turning 180 degrees to right on left foot, legs supple, one step forward with hop on right foot, left leg raised to rear, lowering arms and bringing them up again, right sideward, left forward, obliquely upward. Head to left.

18. Three quick steps left, right, left, lowering arms obliquely sideward and downward.

19. One step forward on toes of right foot and 1/2 turn (180 degrees) to right on right foot with left leg raised sideward, and place it beside right foot, arms sideward, 1/4 turn to right on both feet. . . .

20. Raise right leg to horizontal and thrust it sidward with 5/8 turn to right (225 degrees) on left foot, right arm following motion of right leg.

21. Two running steps, right, left, hop on left foot raising right knee, raise arms sideward and lower, then raise them, forward to horizontal.

22. One step forward with right foot, place right hand on floor, left arm alongside body, turn over forward (one-handed spring) with alternating thrusts of left leg, then right leg, to arrive with weight on left leg.

23. Two steps forward, right, left, thrust right leg forward and upward, left arm rising obliquely sideward and upward, right arm supple in front of body, 1/4 turn to left on left foot.

24. 1/8 turn to left (45 degrees) and one step forward with right foot, bending right knee and bringing left foot on toes behind right foot, leg supple, lowering arms; one step with left left foot to rear and 1/2 turn to right, running step with right foot.

25. Hop on right foot, raising left leg, which is stretched, then bent forward, right arm forward, left arm to rear, extend left leg to rear and kneel, simultaneously lower and raise the arms, left forward, right to rear.

26-27. Shift weight to rear in sitting position on left heel, right leg stretched forward, bend body forward, lowering left arm obliquely to rear, forehead on knees.

28. Straighten up on left knee, right leg stretched forward

with momentary support of left hand on floor, thrust right leg sideward making 3/4 turn to right (270 degrees) on left knee, and place right foot on floor, leg stretched, arms alongside body.

29–30. Bend body to right, raising left arm sideward to form circle over head, right arm sideward and parallel to right leg, head to right.

31. Straighten trunk, lower left arm sideward, bend right leg and place foot in front of left knee, arms crossed in front of body (left on right). Rise to standing position with 1/4 turn to left on right foot, raising left leg forward, arms sideward, palms down.

32. Two fast *chassé* steps, left, right, close feet (left foot slightly in front of right foot), arms obliquely to rear.

33. Immediate complete turn to left with jump, landing on toes, left foot slightly in front of right foot.

34. Hop on left foot, moved obliquely in front of left, thrusting right leg sideward, arms sideward, cross-step with right foot in front of left leg, raising and stretching left leg obliquely to rear, simultaneously raising arms forward from below upward to form circle above head, body extended, head to right.

35. One step with left foot and hop, thrusting right leg and stretching it forward, left arms forward and horizontal, right arm to rear.

36. 1/2 turn to left and land on right foot, hop on right foot thrusting and stretching left leg to rear, left arm forward and horizontal, right arm sideward.

37. 1/2 turn to left and place left foot forward, bring back right leg, first bent, then stretched, and land on right foot, knee supple, simultaneously bend left leg, knee outward, left foot behind right knee, head to right.

38. Hopping, shift from right foot to left foot, extending left knee, land on left foot, knee supple, simultaneously bending right leg, knee outward, right foot behind left knee, head to left.

39. Three hops moving forward toward right (in half-circle) on right leg, bending body to left, arms sideward, left leg stretched to rear.

40. One step with left foot obliquely forward, large lunge to left and 1/2 turn to left on left foot, right leg raised and stretched sideward, arms supple and forward at horizontal, then sit backward at end of turn, left leg bent, right leg stretched forward.

41. Roll to rear, thrusting right leg, then left leg, which is raised obliquely and stretched upward, to land on right knee, simultaneously placing arms sideward on floor with rapid support from hands on beginning roll.

42. Bring left leg forward, bent, straighten on left foot, step with right foot forward on toes, left leg raised to rear, extend body, bending arms in front of body, elbows downward, then stretched, right upward, palm out; left sideward, head to rear. '*Temps* 1/2. *Arrêt* 3.' (Pause)

43. Shift left foot with 3/8 turn to right (135 degrees), cross-step with right foot behind left leg, lowering right arm to horizontal, left arm to rear, shift body to rear 1/2 turn to left on toes of right foot, step forward with left foot, slight body twist to right, arms sideward.

44-45. Step forward with right foot, leg bent, circling of rounded right arm around body, forward, left, to rear, right. Left arm sideward simultaneously extending leg forward with body extended to rear.

46. Shift weight on right leg, once again bent, 3/4 turn to left (270 degrees) on toes of right foot, leg stretched, left leg bent, knee outward, left foot touching right calf, arms rounded in front of body.

47. Sideward extension of left leg and cartwheel to left.

48. Step with left foot to left, with 1/2 turn to left on left foot, lowering arms.

49. Step with right foot to right, raising arms sideward, 1/2 cartwheel to right into handstand.

50-51. Pause.

52. Turn over to rear, thrusting left leg, then right leg, place right foot forward.

53. Step forward with left foot and 3/8 turn to left (135 degrees) on left foot, lowering arms, hop on left foot, thrusting right leg to rear with circling of right arm from rear to front in front of body, left arm sideward.

54. Step to rear with 1/2 turn to right on right foot, lowering right arm forward to horizontal, hop forward on left foot, raising right knee forward and lowering left arm, then bringing it up again forward to the vertical.

55. Round-off on right foot, thrusting with left leg, and landing on both feet.

56. Hop with 1/2 turn to right, land on left foot, right leg raised obliquely forward and downward.

57. Place hands on floor (hand spring), thrusting alternately with left leg, then right leg, to land on left leg.

58. Two steps forward, right, left, lowering arms obliquely sideward and to rear, a large step with right leg, bringing up left leg, simultaneously form circle with right arm sideward and to the outside in front of body, and lower arms.

Uneven parallel bars

1. From side-stand rearways in the middle and in front of lower bars, L-grip, body forward, arms stretched.

2. By bending and stretching the body rearways, assume side sitting position on lower bar.

3. One turn forward (forward seat circle), change hands to upper grip on upper bar.

4. Upstart to straight front support on upper bar and immediately . . .

5. Pass the bent legs between the grip to standing position on lower bar.

6. Change to L-grip on upper bar, bend the legs and body forward and dislocate backward through straight hang, swing forward and rotate backward to support, shifting grips on lower bar to front support.

7. Swing and jump with 1/2 turn to left to squat position on lower bar, change upper grip alternately on high bar.

8. Dismount executing rear vault to left with 1/2 turn over high bar and towards the bar, touching upper bar with grip, change to outer cross-stand (right side toward bar).

Side-horse vault

(Vault No. 11) Straight body ascent, handstand 1/4 turn pivot cartwheel.

Balance beam

From cross-stand frontways at end of beam:

1. Several running steps, with double take-off, place hands on beam, roll forward and come to straight stand on right leg, left leg stretched backward, simultaneously lower arms forward and raise supplely to sideward position, palms downward.

2. One step with left foot, throw right leg forward and jump forward to squat position on toes, arms straight ahead, oblique, rounded, and lowered; with trunk slightly inclined spring up to stand on right leg, arms sideward, left leg stretched backward.

3. One step forward with left foot, 'cat' jump and land on right foot, left foot pointing forward, simultaneously move rounded arms from front to back, oblique and lowered.

4. Place left foot forward, take 1/2 turn to the left, right leg bent with knee outward, toes against left leg, arms downward and slightly rounded, fingers against legs. Immediately place right foot forward, weight of body in that leg, toes of left foot behind right heel, in half-bent position, bend body slightly forward and twist to the left, right arm obliquely forward and downward, left arm rearward and obliquely upward.

5. Lean on left foot to rear, lowering left arm, weight on left leg, rise on left toes while bending, then, extending right leg forward, simultaneously raise arms obliquely forward and up, palms forward.

6. Alternating steps forward, *pas chassé* right, left, right, lowering arms sideward, then bring them up again to horizontal, thrust left leg forward with 1/2 turn to right, simultaneously lower arms, then bring them up again to sideward position, immediately thrust left leg forward.

7. Go down to sitting position, bending right leg, with left leg stretched forward, roll backward bringing stretched legs together with hand grip behind head and come into squat position on right foot, left leg stretched backward, then bring left foot forward, leg bent, body slightly inclined, arms horizontal, palms downward.

8. Assume stretched position on toes, back supple, left foot forward, then lower arms and bring them up again to sideward position.

9   Handstand straddle
lever down to stand   (*Top*)

10, 11   Two balances from the
World Games set work
(*Bottom*)

12 Cartwheel
to handstand
(*Top left*)

13 Handstand
(*Top centre*)

14 Handstand
split position
(*Top right*)

15 Leg lever
through
(*Bottom left*)

16 Leg passing
between
hands to sit
in straddle
position
(*Bottom right*)

9. Thrust leg forward and land on right foot, bring toes of left foot back behind right heel, thrust feet apart, jump and land again on right foot, left leg stretched backward, simultaneously form upward circle with left arm in front of body, right arm sideward.

10. Thrust left leg forward and land on left foot, bring toes of right foot behind left heel, thrust feet apart to jump and land again on left foot, right leg stretched backward, simultaneously form upward circle with right arm in front of body, left arm sideward.

11. Thrust right leg forward, spring up and land with legs supple, right foot forward, left backward, immediately hop, reversing feet, arms sideward, immediately hop and land on right leg, thrusting left leg backward (balance stand frontways), simultaneously form circle with arms from front to back, obliquely (3 seconds). *Hold.*

12. Bring body up, arms sideward, bend right leg placing left leg stretched backward, toes on beam, twist body to left, left arm sideward, right arm supple in front of body, parallel to left arm.

13. Immediately make 1/2 turn to the right, with sideward swing of right arm, and thrust of stretched left leg to return toes to beam.

14. Continue with 1/4 turn to right, bringing left foot back in front of right foot, in squat position, arms horizontal; immediately take 1/2 turn to right (spiral), coming up on toes, left foot backward, arms downward, and bring them up sideward, palms down.

15. Lower arms and bring them back up to horizontal; thrusting stretched left leg forward place left foot forward, momentary handstand, thrusting right leg, then left leg; 1/4 turn left in shifting right hand and dismount with 1/2 turn to cross stand right.

E

3

The Olympic Beam

This piece of apparatus has always been regarded as purely advanced equipment by physical educationists in this country. This can be true but it need not necessarily be so. This is definitely not the case on the Continent, where the beam is used by all ages, the work being planned to suit the requirements of the individual age groups. As a result, the children grow up accepting the beam as part of the P.E. equipment and the tag 'fear beam' is never attached as it is in England. This tag is attached primarily because the beam is put into use at around the age of eleven when almost everything which confronts the child at this age is new: new school, new teachers, new lessons and even new equipment.

The beam can be put into use very successfully along with other equipment. It provides another experimental surface on which to work because it is similar to the balance side of Swedish beams still found in most of our gymnasia except that the working surface is four inches wide across (approx.) and the beam is more stable because of its pedestal stands. These do not require any wedges to maintain equilibrium.

The Olympic beam provides adequate means for interpreting themes requiring different levels at which to work because it can be raised to 3 ft. 11 in. Olympic height and dropped to as little as 2 ft. 6 in. for beginners. Sequences of work can be planned, especially if more than one beam is available—e.g. one beam at 3 ft. 11 in., another at 3 ft. and a third at 2 ft. 6 in. In conjunction with these balancing surfaces, forms can be built up at varying heights and the more timid girls in the class can progress from forms to beam. A floor beam is a very useful addition to any gymnastic equipment and such a beam can be acquired for about £2 to £3. The requirements are a piece of wood 4 in. wide, 6 in. deep and 16 ft. long—planed and sandpapered. Then across the non-working surface a piece of stout wood approximately 2 ft. 6 in. long should be screwed down at both ends. The beam then rests on these legs, lifting the undersurface beam clear of the floor. This is necessary to allow a grip under the beam. Such a floor beam may be stored quite easily at one end of the gym. Heel rubbers should be attached to the supporting wood to prevent damage to the gym floor, also to prevent sliding on a polished surface. Many of our school gymnastic clubs progressed to Olympic work on home-made equipment—indeed, the majority still use improvised apparatus, and will continue to do so until finance is such that correct equipment may be bought.

In conjunction with other P.E. equipment the beam provides another piece of apparatus for confidence training. The actual nature of the beam is in itself suggestive of the type of work which can be achieved on it, but feats of movement performed on the beam nowadays leave very little about which we could say: 'That couldn't be done on a beam.' In advanced beam work, rolls similar to those done on the floor are common on the beam. Weight-bearing movements, such as handstands, cartwheels, back and forward bends, are becoming as frequent as rolls were a few years ago. The standard is rising so rapidly that we in Britain catch up a step only to find that we are several moves behind. But this is at top level and it is with the younger school-child that we are primarily concerned at this moment. To go back to arrangement of equipment in a gym: The beam, because of its length, offers the opportunity for several girls to work at once—jumping over it, springing on to and off it, balancing on it and circling over and under it. Because of the probable nature of the beam it is invaluable in schools where there is only a hall or even a playground. The beam dismantles and assembles very rapidly and it can be the task of a team of youngsters to carry and assemble a beam—under supervision at first of course.

Most children have the inborn tendency to try to walk along fences and walls, so here is the medium for developing the innate urge and training courage at the same time, because there is no doubt that to progress along something high and narrow demands physical courage of many youngsters. The beam is an ideal piece of apparatus for themes demanding partner work, especially if there is more than one beam available. The length of the beam being as it is suggests sequences of movements which can be performed from and to the other. Here, also, is the opportunity for using music, because it helps to produce rhythm and improve balance. This is so because the urge to keep in time with the music is great, therefore the effort to stay on the beam is greater.

As a piece of vaulting equipment the beam also comes into its own. Let me take an isolated vault, a short-arm or bent-arm otherthrow, as an example. The beam allows three people to vault at the same time—two running in one direction and one in another (with small children, as many as four can be accommodated). If the vault is such that the children require a stand-by, then three others can stand by at the beam. In this way six children are active at once. If the children do not require help, then groups of six are vaulting once out of every twice, or if there are nine in the group then once out of every three vaults. If the class is using the whole amount of apparatus freely, i.e. not in groups, then the same thing applies, especially if more than one beam is in use. For some movements it is ideal to coach the whole class at the same time, i.e. to isolate a movement and coach it to everyone, e.g. sitting and standing on the beam. This activity is not nearly so simple as it sounds because of the narrowness of the beam. Sitting freely can be taught on the floor, progressed to forms and then on to beams. Those not ready for the beam can continue on the forms. In this way the whole class is kept active at the same time and yet it allows for individual progress on difficulties.

Confidence training can develop in school lessons long before specific beam work is attempted.

To help the specialist P.E. teacher I have tried to treat this piece of Olympic equipment as I treat it in my own school, i.e. as part of all school equipment. It is just as common for the girls to get out the beams as it is the boxes for vaulting or the ropes for rhythmic skipping.

I have divided the chapter in a similar way to that on agility, but with additions of course. The order in which they appear does not necessarily imply that they should be coached in this way particularly.

1. Beam 'musts'.
2. Progressions of dancing steps.
3. Springs from the beam to return to it.
4. Sitting and lying, also kneeling positions.
5. Rolling movements.
6. Mounts $\left. \right\}$ with or without spring.
7. Dismounts
8. Balance positions.
9. Spins and turns.
10. Advanced agility movements on the beam where body weight is borne on the hands, including movements requiring a great degree of mobility.

1. *'Musts' on the beam*

Because work on the beam is primarily balance it is necessary to discover the easiest way to remain on the beam safely and without undue wobbling. This can be achieved only by complete extension of the body throughout, similar to that of a well-trained ballet dancer. The trunk must be in a permanent state of tension, more especially round the diaphragm, so that the upper trunk feels as though it is being lifted away from the lower. There should be the feeling that the sternum or breast bone is pointing upwards instead of forward. Added to this tremendous trunk extension, the head should maintain a good postural position so that the gymnast feels that she is 'looking down her nose'. The body weight should be kept directly over the feet and the legs should preserve the same extension as the trunk, but with the difference that the knees and ankles should be resilient when required, otherwise harsh landings will result. The gymnast may be told to lean back a little if the style is such that she apparently leans forward. In this way an upright position will be achieved. The arms should be used for regaining balance as naturally as possible and they are a vital preparation of spins and turns; once more they should have movement quality similar to that of a dancer because on the beam arm movements lend grace and flow to the actual dancing steps.

Finally a word or two about foot placing on the beam. Until quite recently we have used the foot-placing method whereby the line of the foot followed the line of the beam, but on watching Continental gymnasts this has proved our approach to be wrong. They use an exaggerated turn-out of the feet, especially on springs, lunge movements and balances from an agility. The beam is gripped strongly by the toes and the instep is regarded as an anchor. When two feet are placed so on the beam, with the toes of the left foot gripping the beam on the left and with the toes of the right foot gripping to the right, then a double anchor is produced. This fixed base is used very strongly in landing from cartwheels and similar movements. It can be seen also that by placing the feet in such a way it minimizes the actual spins or turns because the grounded foot is halfway there.

2. Movements which require poise and balance whilst moving along the beam—i.e. progressions of dancing steps

Beam progressions or simple dancing steps or sequences are of great value in teaching flow along the beam. They serve as a yardstick to the gymnast who can progress along the beam many times without faulting or falling off.

Single progressions

(a) Walk along the beam in very good style, bearing all the beam 'musts' in mind and taking care to extend the toes before gripping the beam. This is a very good exercise in control and basic deportment, also an opportunity for the coach to notice any slight postural deformities.

(b) Make tiny running steps along the beam, trying to run as many steps as possible. Point the toes rapidly before each foot touches the beam, only to push away again just as rapidly. Trunk extension should be maintained and the arms used naturally either working in an easy pattern or simply held outstretched for balance. Stress here should be on ankle resilience and toe extension.

(c) The same as (b) but flick the feet behind. This tends to make the trunk lean forward, so special mention of it should be made.

(d) In all these steps of a dancing nature the aim is to get up from the beam so that the steps look as easy as they would on the floor. To begin the basic spring from the beam, a step, close, step, hop allows the feeling with the stress in the hop. Once confidence is gained this step can be performed along the beam without any worry of overbalancing if the beam 'musts' have been trained throughout.

(e) Step-hops take a further progression and the opportunity for an arm pattern is provided. The gymnast herself will start to use her arms when she feels sure of her feet. The step-hop can be taken with an alternatively bent-knee or a straight-leg lift. The bent-knee lift provides a contrast for a straight-leg turn; as the gymnast becomes more proficient two or three steps can be joined together so that two beam lengths may comprise three or more steps.

(f) The feather step often provides the gymnast with a mental task in gymnastics as well as physical. This step requires two hops on the same foot, whilst the other foot is thrown backward from the knee on the first hop, then forward from the knee on the second hop. A useful coaching point is 'bend stretch'. The bend stretch is repeated alternately on each foot. Once again this can be linked to other steps, e.g. feather, feather, hop one, two, three, i.e. two feather steps and a polka.

(g) Children skip from a early age, so a skipping step along the beam provides them with a medium that they already know. Confident skippers may even try to use a rope, but care should be taken that the skipper starts far enough from the end so that the rope does not catch. This ability to leave the beam for the rope to pass under the feet is very good training for tucks and springs on the beam.

(h) Now, most of the steps are progressions forwards, but of course they can be altered by travelling sideways. Slip steps provide a good beginning. Slip, turning to the left, beginning with right foot, then repeat, turning to the right with the left foot. One or two steps have been mastered, then the gymnasts can develop their own ideas, possible working in twos and keeping in time.

(i) Many Scottish dancing steps provide a good start

for beam professions and some of the simple Highland steps can add interest to those steps already known.

(j) Throughout these steps the arms should be encouraged to move naturally and sometimes forwards or backwards as the step suggests. As soon as possible they should start to feel movements, experimenting with the space above, to the side and behind. The arms should also be helped to move one in one direction and one in another so that asymmetric movements are as easily performed as symmetric.

These suggestions leave a sufficient leeway for the teacher of P.E. to plan her own scheme of work. National dancing provides many unusual steps, whilst ballet can provide those of a very definite technique also. Sufficient scope is also given for the imagination of the individual gymnast to prepare, select and define her own movement requirements. It is in such work that modern dance has much to offer the gymnast because the training in movement will add interest to otherwise single steps.

3. *Movements which require spring from the beam and the ability to return to it*

These are the kinds of movements which test the gymnast's balance to the utmost, because here she must be able to leap off the beam and return to it as surely as to the floor in order to go into another movement. Springing freely from the sides and ends of the beam gives the feeling of foot-thrust which is essential, but as soon as possible springs from and back to again should be attempted, no matter how small the spring. It is amazing the progress which can be made in perfecting a movement or spring by making twenty or thirty attempts; at first only a few will be successful, but as practice is continued the mind and body become attuned to the task in hand and success becomes greater.

(a) *A leaping step along the beam.* This can be started simply by trying to spring from one foot on to the other in a progression along the beam. Gradually the spring will increase, then the length of the spring can be increased too. The leading leg should be lifted well up in front of the body and at the same time the foot-thrust of the other leg should propel the body forwards and upwards at the same time. An obstacle placed on the beam often gives the initial feeling of leaping over something. A leap is just a single movement, and so once it is mastered thought should be given as to how it may be linked with a further movement or from where it may have been derived. A progression on a straight leap is that of a stag leap where the front leg is bent up first then stretched out before landing.

(b) *Springing up to change feet in the air.* The feet should be placed one in front of the other close together and turned out. The spring is developed from a slight give in the knees, allowing the knees to straighten in the air. At the same time both feet thrust away the beam and while in the air the feet change so that on landing the other foot comes to rest in front. This spring can be done many times changing feet and many times leaving the feet in the same position. The resilience of knees and feet allow the extension to be replaced when arriving on the beam. In this spring the arm may be used to help the spring or simply to form a balance position. Different speeds can be introduced to add interest, i.e. two spring changes to stay in the air as long as possible, followed by two or three very quick changes in which the spring is hardly noticeable.

(c) *Tuck jump.* This is very similar to the spring hop in that the spring arises from two feet at the same time and the weight is pushed directly upwards. Here, though, the feet do not change in the air and the spring is much greater. Also, the knees are drawn up to the chin to give a 'true tuck effect'. The feet are placed one in front of the other for take-off and they land in the same position, though with the body weight more on the front foot. The arms can help a great deal in this jump. The tuck is very effective, especially if it is followed by another jump of a similar nature, i.e. tuck jump followed by a splits jump.

(d) *Splits jump*. In this the feet are thrust apart very rapidly from the same position as in the tuck. The legs should achieve a splits in the air, both back and forward leg stretched to capacity. Here again the body weight should be kept over the front foot and the trunk held upright. The arms may help in the lift of the body or they may strike a poise suitable to the splits jump.

(e) Another jump is that of the *stag jump*. Once again take-off and landing positions are the same, but the spring goes directly upwards. At the same time the back leg achieves splits whilst the front one is bent at the knee with the foot completing the line of the extended back leg. This is a very interesting spring but not easy to achieve because of the asymmety of the movement.

(f) *Straddle jump sideways*. This jump is a star jump from the beam back on to the beam. The feet may be placed side by side for the jump, but it is necessary to land with one foot in front of the other because of the narrowness of the beam.

(g) *A scissor kick*. A scissor step on a high jump spring may be performed along the beam with take-off from one foot on to the other. The thrust from one foot lifts the body weight upwards and at the same time the free leg should go as high as possible. The thrusting leg then becomes the kicking leg and so the scissor-like action is completed. This step can be varied so that a scissor action from one foot is completed but the landing is on two feet, body in a crouching position. Similarly, a two-foot spring may be developed so that after the upwards spring the weight is borne on one foot only.

(h) *Gallop step or comat.* This is exactly the same action as in the scissor step, but in this case the knee is bent and the leg is lifted high with the knee leading. The lower leg is kept extended in preparation for landing. Comat steps are very useful as dancing steps along the beam because they can either flow into another movement or by retarding the second knee lift they can provide a good opportunity for regaining stillness before a spin or even terminate as a lunge. These steps provide interest for variation of arm movements. Commonly the gallop step is used with an arm circling forward so that the trunk inclines forward with head towards the knees, but of course the arms may be used in several other ways, e.g. arm circling backwards, which produces a very upright body position, or arms to lift sideways into ring overhead and return through the same space pattern to the sides of the body. Individuals will find many variations and it is by these ideas that pleasing voluntary work arises.

There are other springs from the beam, but mainly they are methods of dismounting or mounting and they will be dealt with under a different section.

4. *Sitting, lying and kneeling positions*

All the work on the beam has so far been in the nature of an upright position which traverses the beam. Now we experiment with other parts of the body besides landings on the feet. The beam being so narrow, only four inches wide, it may seem impossible to lie, sit and kneel with apparent safety, but it can be done satisfactorily, because, as in everything else, practice makes perfect and what at first seemed impossible becomes very probable. Wobbling and shaking accompanies the first attempts to lie, sit and kneel on the beam and it is here that a floor beam is extremely useful. It is only a few inches above the floor and if mats are placed underneath then the gymnast can fall off quite happily, but, strangely enough, falls are not nearly so numerous as would be expected. Once an experienced gymnast works on the beam at championship height she hates to work it lower. The incentive to stay on the beam, i.e. the height, is taken away, but for beginners a low beam is ideal.

FIG. 15

Sitting on the beam

(a) Sit astride the beam, i.e. with both feet pointing down to the floor, maintain this position and take the hands away from the beam. Lift the arms sideways, above the head, and lower them again. If the legs and trunk are kept truly stretched then very little wobbling will result. From this position place both hands on the beam behind the seat. A standing position can be formed from this preparatory squat-up.

(b) *Squat-up*. This is one of the most useful methods of alighting on the beam from a sitting position astride the beam. The legs are raised forward and the hands placed close in to the body in front. The legs are then swung backwards strongly, but without flexion. The seat must be lifted clear of the beam; to do this the weight of the body is borne by the hands through the shoulders. The feet are brought up on to the beam in close relation to the hands, so that the finished movement is that of a crouching position. With greater extension of the legs and piking at the hips, together with greater forward strength, a straight-leg squat may be achieved, i.e. the knees stay straight throughout from the swing to standing on the beam.

(c) *Sitting on the beam from standing*. This method whereby one leg is kept straight and the other bent until the seat touches the beam is so simple for anyone with supple ankles and long tendon achilles that it may seem unnecessary to mention it, but for the gymnast who lacks this great degree of flexion at the ankles it offers a great obstacle. In order to be able to sit smoothly the weight of the body must not transfer itself over either the front leg or over the seat. It must be kept exactly over the standing foot. The actual sit: Stand erect on one foot with the other extended forward at right angles. Now keep that position by sliding the lifted leg down the inside of the one which is to bend. In this way the sit can be controlled. The body should not lean forward or backward to compensate. This exercise should be practised on the floor and on forms many times until the position has been achieved. Many gymnasts will sit like this without even thinking twice. A useful method is for a stand-by to give a little manual help until the feeling for the movement is acquired. Similarly from this position a stand can be practised simply by straightening the bent leg. It is very necessary, though, to make sure that all these movements are practised on both legs, because in a piece of 'set work' choice of leg may not be given.

(d) *Sit on the beam in riding seat*. This is a sideways position on the beam where one leg is extended and the other bent at the knee so that the side-saddle riding seat is shown. From here the bent leg may be straightened and lifted over the beam. Now the straddle-sit position is shown again. Place the hands behind the seat and lean back slightly. With a smooth movement lift both legs up in front of the body so that a 'v' sit position is made. The legs should go as close to the nose as possible before one leg is bent and the foot placed on the beam. A quick transfer of weight from seat and hands over the standing foot should result in an upright position. All the body weight should go forward to stand. The arms can extend forward, too, to help the standing position.

(e) *Progressions from sitting to lying on the back*. From the straddle-sit position the legs should be lifted up together and placed on the beam. The back should be rounded so that each part of the spine touches the beam as back-lying position is achieved. The hands should be taken slowly above the head to grip the beam on its under surface. Bracing of the elbows, strengthening in the shoulderstand, gripping tightly with the fingers, all give the necessary tenseness required to hold the body firmly along the beam. At the same time body and leg extension should be kept. A useful practice is to lift the legs clear of the beam, gradually reaching 90 degrees, then even farther until the toes touch the beam above the head. In this folded position the beginning of a backward roll is felt. From back-lying position the gymnast can experiment with ways of changing to sitting, i.e. to astride, to stand, to squat-up and into riding seat. A similar back-lying can be tried but with the hand placed down the side of the beam. By this method it is possible to see the part of the beam above the head (preparation for back roll).

(f) *Front-lying* is used very rarely on the beam in exercises but it can be used as an alternative to back-lying for experimental purposes. If the hands are placed under the beam one leg can be lifted by pulling on the hands. The free leg can be bent and placed under the knee of the lifted leg. A pleasing balance may result on one knee and hands if the back is arched to give line to the movement.

(g) *Kneeling*. Another part of the body which is used for weight-bearing on the beam. It is a useful means of completing a roll, i.e. on to one or two knees. At first it is not easy to balance on the knees because of their round-ness, but with the hands to assist at first, balancing becomes easier. The squat-up on to the beam, taken earlier, can be altered slightly so that one knee is placed on the beam instead of two feet. A knee spin can also be practised, i.e. to face in the other direction. This should be well practised on forms and on the floor before being attempted at a height. The body weight should be kept over the shoulders rather than over the knee. Starting positions are one knee on the beam, free leg lifted behind both hands on the beam in front of knee. With a little preparatory movement, swing the free leg round and spin on the knee. The hands release the beam and come to rest again when the 180 degrees have been turned by the body.

5. *Rolling movements forwards and backwards*

These rolls should be perfected on the floor and on forms before putting them on to the beam, because there is the similarity of rolling and the necessary grip from the forms.

Rolling forwards

(a) A forward roll to stand can be achieved in exactly the same way as one does on a mat but is an advanced movement. A similar roll is that of a small spring to take weight on hands, then, as soon as the head is tucked in and the weight transferred to the shoulders, the hands should change their grip from on top of the beam to underneath. This is the 'check' of the roll speed, i.e. the method of braking. The speed of the legs is slowed down too so that they either finish at 'L's to the beam or parallel to the beam, but the latter with control. The back should not be thrust at the beam, nor should it be kept flat. In the same way as on the floor, the spine should be rounded, but only until the grip is put into action. With a floor beam these rolls can be tried unsupported, but it is wise to have help when using a high

17 J. Nicholson emulates
the champion (*Top left*)
18 Stag handstand
(*Top right*)
19 Split handstand
(*Bottom*)

beam. If the gymnast feels that she is falling off to the side of the beam a little shoulder spring can be executed. This brings the feet to the floor and the gymnast lands the right way up.

(b) When the forward roll is mastered it can be developed into a dive roll, i.e. to show a space between the beam and hands and feet before the hands touch.

(c) Similarly, another progression is that of a similar dive roll, but the grip is put into action only for a second. Immediately the gymnast should try to stand up with one foot in front of the other. There is little danger of missing the beam because it is a sighted landing. Although the body curls in the air, it must be a controlled curl, and as soon as it rests on the beam full extension must take over. This applies even more strongly if a roll to stand is attempted. The stand itself provides the check—every fibre must be extended to control the speed of the roll, because the roll will be only one movement in a series of many, probably the simplest, therefore full control is needed throughout.

(d) *Continuing with the ensuing movement.* To progress even further, a dive roll along the beam can be executed without altering the grip on the beam, i.e. hands placed on the top of the beam and left there long enough to take the weight of the body. This roll does not demand height but forward speed. The feet are placed one in front of the other to stand and they should be turned out to grip the beam.

Rolling backwards

(a) The simplest backward roll is that on to one knee from back-lying with the head at the side of the beam. There is no hard-and-fast rule as to which side the head should be or how the hands should be placed. A gymnast with short limbs will invariably place one hand on top of the beam and one underneath. This is quite a good way,

F

because it gives the pull for the initial roll and the push for the finishing position. Many gymnasts prefer both hands under the beam because they form a double grip, while others place both hands on the top. Whichever way the gymnast finds most satisfactory should be used. The backward roll on to one knee should pass almost through and should stand with both legs extended. This lifts the weight upwards. One leg should be bent and placed on the beam (feel it with the top of the foot and look at the place). This is one roll where safety should be certain because each slip can be seen. Once the knee is in place the weight should be pushed backwards to take it from the hands. This allows the gymnast to stand. An important point in this roll is to show clearly the split of the legs, i.e. one leg pulling in one direction and one in another. This acts as balance and a lever.

(b) Another roll can be practised which is similar to (a), in that as far as a shoulderstand it is the same, except that the lift to it must be faster. From here the weight is pushed forward and the back arched, i.e. the beam apparently slides down the front of gymnast from sternum to hips (chest roll). The final position is to finish sitting astride the beam. The legs should be kept up off the beam as long as possible until the chest roll is completed. By doing thus the legs will not come down with speed and scrape along the beam.

(c) *Backward roll with head placed on the beam.* This resembles a backward roll done on the floor, in that the head is not avoided but left in a natural position. This backward roll is much more difficult than (a) and (b) because the landing on the beam is blind. Therefore it is necessary to produce a roll which does not deviate from a straight line at all. From back-lying, hands placed above the head (both hands on top or underneath the beam), quickly lift the legs with such speed that the roll passes over the top of the head. Once again feel for the beam with the foot while the free leg is kept high in the air. Once the free leg starts to drop the whole roll becomes more chancy. The hands must push away evenly to enable the head to lift into a finished position.

(d) *Backward roll on to foot*. Same approach as for (c) but a quicker lift of the legs upwards; one leg stays up high whilst the other leg bends to place the foot on the beam. Once again the roll goes over the top of the head. The hands must push away from the beam very rapidly. From landing on one foot the free leg may extend backwards to balance on the beam. It may be swung forward to rest on the beam or it may be swung forward and backward to lift the body weight up to stand. An advanced movement from this landing is to swing into handstand.

(e) *Backward roll to headstand*. This is a difficult movement to do and one not used very much because it is not particularly elegant for a girl to do. The hands must be placed side by side on top of the beam. Usually the roll commences from sitting to give extra impetus, but it can be done from back-lying. The legs must lift very rapidly upwards and backwards (aim for a handstand). The hands take an equal part of the weight, i.e. half on the head and half on the hands. The legs and trunk must be braced strongly in order to maintain balance.

All these rolls are based on fundamental principals applying to rolls on the floor, but because they are done on the beam the necessary fixing of a point, i.e. the hands above the head, alters the actual movement. The pattern becomes roll, stop, finish, whereas on the floor a roll is much more continuous. This pattern of stop, go can fit into a theme of speeds very satisfactorily, especially as these rolls are mostly determined as 'bound flow'. Some of the forward rolls where no grip is used allow for the much freer type of flow which gathers speed.

Finally on rolls, one which is rather simple is the backward roll to slide out to a flat position. The head is placed at the side of the beam, the legs lifted deliberately up-wards, then the top of both feet laid together on the beam above the head. The feet then slide away from the body until the trunk and legs are extended. Press down on the beam with the hands until the trunk is arched. From here both legs may swing off the beam so that the body is in an upright position, toes pointing to the ground. Once again the gymnast has arrived in an astride position from which she can select her own method of mount or dismount.

6. *Mount—methods of arriving on the beam*

Springs from two feet

(a) Spring to hip-rest across the beam by placing both hands (fingers forwards) on the beam. A good line from head to toe should be shown before progressing to the method chosen for standing erect.

(b) *Squat on the beam.* With a short run, place both hands on the beam (fingers forward) and spring up from both feet to place them between the hands on the beam. The seat must lift and the spring be fast, otherwise the knees will scrape the beam. If the hands are too wide the squat will not be successful because there will not be sufficient height for the bent legs. If the gymnast finds the squat is difficult it may be either that she is not lifting at the hips or that she is not carrying her weight forward over her hands. The arms must be kept straight. To achieve a straight-leg squat the hips must lift very much higher first, then a quick pike at the hips follows. The weight travels much farther forward over the shoulders and hands.

(c) A progression on this is a *squat-over to sit*. The same approach is made but the squat is slowed down. The feet must lift clear of the beam and the legs stretch out. The body almost pivots on the shoulders because the hips are completely clear of the beam. Once the legs are straight the seat should be placed on the beam, and a good extended body position shown before mounting the beam to stand.

(d) *Straddle on to the beam*. The same take-off from two feet with the hands placed forward on the beam. The seat must lift very high if a narrow straddle is required, but if splits position is good then the seat need not lift up so much. The weight must pass over the beam outside the hands. The tendency is to straddle straight over so that the hands can be used as a fixed point by placing the fingers forward and the thumbs behind. This provides a grip. From the straddle position the body may turn into a lunge or turn on to one knee.

(e) *Straddle-over to sit*. This is similar in approach to the squat through to sit, except that the legs pass outside the hands. The legs are delayed and the seat kept clear of the beam. All the weight is borne on the hands placed the same as for straddle. The shoulders are well forward. From here the seat may be placed on the beam or kept clear until a quarter- or half-turn is made; the legs stay in straddle above the beam and the body turns for a quarter-turn; the hands remain still, but for a half-turn the left hand must move alongside the right if the turn is to the left and vice versa if the turn is to the right.

(f) *Short arm or bent arm to shoulderstand*. This is a spring from two feet into a shoulderstand across the beam. The hands must be placed forward, not with the thumbs behind the beam. From the spring the body lifts into a piked position, which is maintained by the shoulders and hips, but the legs are slowly lifted. Once the upright is achieved the back may be hollowed a little. Two or three ways for continuing from the shoulder are possible. 1. Maintain the body position, but lift up from the shoulder and slide down to hip-rest. 2. Make a quarter-turn and sit astride the beam. 3. Make a quarter-turn and place one knee or foot on the beam.

(g) *Short arm on beam lengthways*. This provides a double

take-off from the side of the beam into a shoulderstand. The hands are placed side by side and the weight is borne by one shoulder only. The head lies alongside the beam. Similar positions from the shoulderstand can be found to bring the gymnast on to the beam in a standing position.

(h) *Dive roll on to the end of the beam.* A dive roll of this kind necessitates a sure roll and a confident attack. A board may be used to give the correct take-off position for the feet and to leave sufficient space between the feet and the beam to allow the dive. The spring upwards must be fast and sure, with a good lift of the hips to enable the head to tuck into the neck. The hands should be placed along the beam side by side about a foot from the end. Once the shoulders touch the beam the grasp should be shifted under the beam, as in an ordinary forward roll. This stops the speed of the roll. When the roll is more certain the grip on the beam can become less, to allow the gymnast to stand from a rolling movement. From here the hands need not even grasp the beam. In this case the roll will be continuous along the beam. A fast roll into a static balance makes a good start for a voluntary sequence, i.e. speed-roll with a curl (stretch out into a static balance), showing asymmetry and contrast.

The dive roll can be attempted from the side of the beam with a board for take-off. A very quick change of hand-grasps must be used, with a stronger pull by the hand on the side of take-off.

(i) *Lever up to handstand.* This start is not very common on the beam because it must be performed without apparent strength, i.e. on straight arms; no press-up is allowed in women's work. As a result, the spring from the floor must be great enough for the gymnast to achieve a handstand position with hands and arms and trunk. Once the hips are over the shoulders, the hips are fixed, and on this fixed point the legs are lifted sideways through straddle then brought together. It is not important that the trunk remains still and extended to allow the legs to lever on the trunk. Numerous possibilities can arise from a handstand but these will be dealt with under the chapter of more difficult agility.

Springs from one foot to mount the beam

(a) From a sideways approach, place the nearest hand on the beam, spring from one foot farthest from the beam on to the inside foot, which has been lifted up in front in order to stand on it. A step, close, step can be used for the run or simply a few steps run. The hand on the beam helps to give a little thrust. Once the first foot is on the beam the trunk should be straightened and the other foot placed along the beam. (Mount pattern: Run from the left place, left hand on beam, spring off right foot on to left, lift on to beam. Stand erect. The weight should be carried directly over the standing foot or taken forward.

(b) The same spring from one foot can be used at the end of the beam, but the take-off board must allow enough space for the first leg to lift clear, without actually touching the beam. In this mount no hands are used, therefore the spring must be sufficient to alight on the beam in an erect stance.

(c) Fencing rear vault supplies another means of mounting the beam from one foot. The mount is a rear vault done over the beam from a sideways approach (obliquely to the beam). The near hand is placed on the beam, the near leg lifted over first, followed by the far leg. The second hand grasps the beam after the second leg. The legs must be kept braced, otherwise the body will be forced forward. This happens when the knees bend under the beam in an attempt to remain on the beam. Once again stress should be on a complete extension. Where relaxation is apparent on the beam, the gymnast either falls or wobbles. In the fencing rear to sit on the beam the first leg over is kept straight, the second bent at the knee to give the riding-seat position.

(d) *Their vault as a mount.* This is done facing the beam with the board far enough away to allow for both legs to be lifted one after the other in front of the beam. There must be a snappy start, the legs following each other very quickly through the hands, which have been placed on the beam *after* the legs have passed over it. There is the 'cheat' of time, i.e. when neither hands nor feet touch the beam. The handgrip is such that it stops the forward speed of the vault almost with a jerk and the legs are pressed rapidly against the beam in a riding-seat position. The thumbs provide the strength with which the speed is reduced. The feet and legs do not pass over the beam in such a high position as they would in a vault.

These are some examples of one- and two-footed starts or mounts on the beam around which many others can be developed as the gymnast improves.

7. *Dismounts from the beam which require spring*

Simple jumps make the best introduction to leaping from the beam. They are the kinds of jumps with which the gymnast will probably be familiar from leaping off apparatus and jumping into water as progressions for diving.

The tuck jump can be done from the beam, many girls working at once, three or four jumping from the length of the beam and one leaping from each end. An erect position should be aimed for before jumps are commenced, then the knees brought up to the chin, not the head to the knees. The tuck should be quick and equally so should be the stretch-out before landing; at all times endeavour to keep the trunk straight in the air in order to land in a balanced position. In landing, the ankles and feet should take most of the shock and a little by the knees. Right from the start the gymnast should try to land standing up straight to avoid the 'knee-full-bend' position. This is dangerous when landing from great heights because once the knees are fully flexed there is nothing else left to take any jar which may remain. The feet and ankles should provide the 'give' for landing and if the body is kept high on landing the weight will not be so great as when the whole body relaxes forward. This is particularly so when landing from a handstand from the high bar at 7 ft. 6 in. plus the gymnast's own height.

Similar jumps to the tuck jump are the pike and straddle. In the former the legs are kept together extended, then lifted forward so that a right angle is produced between the body and legs. In the straddle the same position is aimed for, but the legs remain apart. Again the trunk should stay upright and the legs pike at the hips, i.e. flexion at the hip joint, then they extend before landing. The hands many be used to grasp the ankles or touch the toes in the straddle and pike. If a trampoline is available these jumps may be perfected on it. The hollow-back jump has take-off and landing the same as the other jumps, but the arms are thrown above the head while the back hollows and legs extend backwards. From this arched position the body is brought back into line before landing. A short run along the beam may be followed by a single-foot take-off to spring up into the air, then to join the legs together. The impetus should be directed upwards to check the forward momentum.

Once a controlled landing has been achieved, then a spring from the hands may be tried.

(a) *Handspring from the end of the beam*. It is assumed that the gymnast can perform a handspring well on the ground before attempting it on the beam. It is also a good idea to do it from a box which is wider, then off a form at a height, then from the beam which is relatively narrow. A handspring from the beam requires that the arms should be kept straight, the head held back and the speed of the catch-up leg be not too great. Once the spring is felt, then the speed can be increased to produce flight. The hands should touch the beam only briefly, i.e. this is not intended to be a handspring overthrow, but a definite spring.

This spring can also be tried from the side of the beam, placing one hand on only—the same hand as the hopping foot in the handspring. This is so that the spring travels sideways a little to avoid landing on the beam. The hand position can quickly be changed and placed back on the beam to give a sure grip for landing.

Simple dismounts without spring

(a) *Crouch jump from the side of the beam.* From standing position on the beam place both hands at the front of the feet on the beam. Push the seat upwards, thrusting the weight over the shoulders. The hips are turned slightly in a sideways position alongside the beam. After a few attempts the hips can be pushed a little higher and the legs kept straight. This gives a 'hip-hump' position.

(b) *Kick to almost a handstand.* Here the gymnast puts both hands on the beam and kicks up as though going into a handstand, i.e. from one foot at a time. The body does not reach vertical but almost so. The hands are placed close together and side by side. By pushing more strongly from the thrusting foot, the body turns a little sideways to alight. Finish sideways to beam, facing in the direction that the gymnast started.

(c) *Handstand from the end of the beam.* This is a progression on (b) in so much that the verticle is reached, passed through and over to land forming an arc. Both hands are placed near the end of the beam and the elbows must be braced very hard, otherwise tilting to one side will result. The kick up is the same as for a handstand on the floor, but it doesn't stop. All other coaching points for a handstand apply. This dismount is, in effect, a handstand overthrow from the end of the beam. An erect position of the trunk, plus an extension of the shoulder joints, should be aimed for. If this is attained all the way through the handstand then the body is simply turned over. It may be necessary to give a little push from the hands.

(d) *Cartwheel dismount*. This may be treated as a preparation for a cartwheel to handstand and overthrow. The cartwheel position is such that the hands are both placed across the beam, fingers pointing in the same direction—the second hand a few inches from the end of the beam. A sideways position of the body is shown as, for example, the left leg lifts. This is followed by left hand, right hand, right leg, left leg; the legs join together contrary to a real cartwheel. The cartwheel position is maintained by the hands and by the body, not by the legs. Once the legs are together the body wheels on the right hand to land sideways to the beam with right hand touching. The cartwheel should pass through the vertical and the body should complete a sideways arc. If the back is allowed to hollow too much the landing will not be in line with the beam. It is necessary to push off the last hand to enable the body to turn the correct way up. Once again the elbows should be extended, also the trunk and legs. A cartwheel on to one arm makes an effective finish and choice of arms is left to the gymnast, depending on which she finds easier on the floor. The coaching is the same except that the dismount happens more quickly— the wheel is faster and the release and push from the beam is speedier too.

(e) *Cartwheel to handstand and overthrow*. Once the cartwheel finish has been practised, then a cartwheel to handstand in the centre of the beam may be tried. It is wise to have someone standing in for this, because the tendency is for the cartwheel not to stop at handstand at first. *Cartwheel handstand pattern*. Gymnast cartwheeling from the left end of the beam on to right hand first, i.e. cartwheel to handstand, hands shoulder width apart. Stand-in: Face the beam and place left hand under the right shoulder as handstand is felt—place right hand in the small of the back if the handstand is gained, but if the cartwheel looks as though it is going to continue, place the right arm around the body and steady the position. Two stand-ins may be used, in which case the first one takes the right shoulder and the second the left. This will serve to balance the handstand. From here the overthrow is tried. Full extension throughout, and sighting of the landing by using the head, should produce a fairly steady landing. Once extension is lost a crumpled landing results. Eventually the cartwheel to handstand becomes so sure that turns from it can be tried, also straddle and squat position for finishing. In all handstands along the beam the feet should be over the shoulders for balance and the balance should be worked for by controlling the handstand with very small shoulder movements rather than using the legs.

(f) *Handstand quarter-turn down to land*. The handstand position is arrived at from a cartwheel. When the handstand is steady, i.e. in balance, the weight is transferred to one hand, allowing the other to become free of the beam. The body then pivots on the weighted arm (right arm, for example) to the right, to finish standing right side to the beam. The handstand position should be kept the whole time so that a curve remains until landing, when it is lost by the flexion of ankles and knees. *At all times* the head must be kept back and the gymnast should be aware of where she is going. When a handstand on the beam has been learned, numerous possibilities are opened up for the gymnast. She can learn to cartwheel, to handstand and wheel out for a finish; she can do a handstand along the beam and quickly move a hand so that she is in cartwheel position. From there she can choose her own dismount.

Dismounts which may be classed as shoulder levers

(g) *Handstand squat-down.* Handstand position first. The feet must be well over the head but in line. Now the legs are brought down in a squat position between the hands to alight in an upright position. To develop this ability, the gymnast must first definitely feel the handstand. Then the shoulders are allowed to move forward and at this point the legs are whipped down quickly from the hips, between the hands. The hands thrust strongly from the beam when the legs come through to put the body in a landing position. The head must be used very well in these dismounts by being held back and sighting the landing. The legs from the handstand appear to fall over the head, but this is because the shoulders move forward—they should not be allowed to fall over but to keep in line with the body.

(h) *Handstand straight-leg squat.* This is performed in exactly the same way as (g), but the shoulders must move farther forward, the leg whip must be faster and the hips must be allowed to come farther over the head so that a real pike is shown momentarily. The thrust from the hands again puts the body into an alighting position.

(i) *Handstand straddle-down.* All the previous coaching points apply to this also with the exception of the leg position. In this the legs pass round the hands instead of between. They are kept extended and brought together for landing. (More difficult dismounts under the section on advanced agility.)

8. *Balance positions*

These provide the gymnast with the opportunity of selecting a position which she likes to show. All balances should extend from two to three seconds, not a shorter time, otherwise the balance is not clearly defined. Two or three things should be born in mind when selecting balances:

FIG. 16

Which part of the body is going to be used for balancing. Secondly, how the beam is going to be used, i.e. whether stance is across the beam, straight along or obliquely. Thirdly, which balances suit the gymnast best. Of course, the latter does not apply in set work because the gymnast has no choice. Shoulderstands have been included in a previous part, so they will be omitted here and the stress placed on balances on one foot or balances which have a rather more aesthetic quality, i.e. the kind found in dancing.

(a) *Arabesque.* In this balance the gymnast, depending on her suppleness, can place her free leg parallel to the beam, obliquely upwards or even as far as 90 degrees. It may be completely extended, the hip outwardly rotated, or it may be bent at the knee in a definite shape. The higher the leg pattern, the lower the arm pattern should be to give a line from finger-tip to toe. The oblique position, with the arm forward and the other arm back to follow the line of the leg, is a very pleasing one on the beam. This particularly because it is in direct contrast with the very straight practical working surface of the beam. The arabesque may be altered so that it is quite different. The standing leg is braced, the high back leg bent at the knee, the hand grasps the back high leg at the foot to pull it

94

even higher and the free arm points upwards or downwards. If the free arm determines that it shall be downwards, then the whole body tilt results. The head should always be held erect and in balances of this nature, especially, complete extension of the body is vital. If this is carried out, then there need not be even the slightest shake in either limb. Once again the arm positions may be symmetric or asymmetric. Using symmetry, both arms may be extended forwards very close to the beam or parallel to the beam so they may be extended backwards into a line resembling the modern delta-wing planes. In each of these balances it is necessary for the coach to watch carefully and select the most pleasing position on which the gymnast can work. Balances of this nature may be moved into slowly until the line is found then held, or they may be snapped into. This method is used a great deal by the Russian team and perhaps it is from this that they may have had such success. This ability to stop 'dead' gives a terrific opportunity for regaining or maintaining balance.

(b) All of the balances mentioned up to now have been on a straight standing leg. A leg flexed at the knee strongly so that the hip apparently folds (femur on ileum) gives another aeroplane effect. The stance for the balance can be across the beam or obliquely along it.

(c) From standing with weight on one leg, many positions can be shown using variations of arm pattern. Those teachers familiar with modern dance terms can experiment with different planes and some rather unusual balance patterns may result, e.g. with top half of the trunk turned in one direction to produce a twist of the waist or at the shoulders.

(d) The trunk, instead of leaning forward, may be placed in a backward position or extended laterally. These two positions again give a basis for building other types of balances. I have purposely spent little time on this section because, apart from rules on balancing, so much of this kind of work depends on the gymnast and her coach, but I hope that the outline will be sufficient to give a lead along the right lines for development.

9. *Spins, turns and lunges*

Spins and turns are a means of using the length of the beam many times over. A mount followed by a sequence and a dismount would not lead to very interesting work, so the gymnast must learn to turn at the end of the beam or in the centre, depending on what is required. The simplest way to learn to face in the opposite direction is to place both feet, one in front of the other, quite close, rise on the toes, and turn round without actually moving the feet. The feet will spin on the balls. The effort to turn should be from the shoulders and hips once the stretch up has been achieved. These turns can be done by the hundred to the left and the right so that the gymnast feels absolutely at home turning round. The actual turns should be fairly fast and then a 'stop' should follow. The head should turn as a dancer's when performing a spin, i.e. the eyes fixed for as long a time as possible.

180-degree turn on one foot—suggestions for practice and coaching points.

(a) Left spins have been used as examples, but the whole spin should be reversed so that the gymnast is equally versatile. Stand on left foot placed obliquely across the beam, i.e. pointing to the left, turn on this foot at 90 degrees to the left, leaving the right leg free to complete a circle from behind the left foot, round and on to the beam, in front of the left foot.

COACHING: Spin on the ball of the foot placed obliquely, put the heel down to stop the spin—keep the body weight over the spinning foot—body extended and free leg away

24 Position for the start of a dislocation

25 Another starting position for a dislocation

26 Dislocation

27, 28   Starting position for a hock swing   29   Actual hock swing

30   Hock swing to catch with   31   The hock swing half-turn
      half-turn   to catch

from the fixed foot. Use the head to initiate the stop by fixing the eyes and keeping it well in line.

(b) Stand on the right leg, knee braced, foot placed forward. Swing the left leg forward and back—on the back swing the body turns to the left. This is a back spin with the left shoulder leading backwards and round to the left. The left foot may be kept clear of the beam, lifted up and bent so that a balance results, or placed on the beam in front, e.g. the right foot.

COACHING: Same as for (a) but attempt to lean back slightly after the first swing.

(c) Spin standing on the left foot to the left by swinging the right leg forward, then bending it at the knee so that the outside of the right leg lies against the outside of the left leg. Turn to the left in this position, i.e. with right leg bent. The right leg should swing into this bent position to give the impetus for the spin.

COACHING: Complete extension of the trunk and limbs until the moment of flexion of the right leg. Spin on the ball of the foot and keep right foot extended.

(d) *Back spin.* Stand on the right leg with left foot in front just touching the beam. Lift the left leg and cross it over the right leg. Now circle the left leg to the left a full 360 degrees so that it finishes behind the right foot on the beam. In this spin the body turns 190 degrees, but the left leg completes a 360-degree turn.

COACHING: The left leg should be regarded as a free leg in balance, i.e. to make it stay clear of the beam. It is the driving leg to initiate the turn.

In all of these turns the arms play an important part in aiding the turn and in stabilizing it once the turn is made. If the spin is to the left then the arms prepare to the right in order to give momentum to the spin.

Once turns of 180 degrees are mastered then it is just a matter of practice to develop then into 360-degree turns and even more. It is useful to attempt a 360-degree

G

spin using the free foot as a pivot until the body adjusts itself to the extra turn. Extra half- and quarter-turns can be added at will so that a free-leg 180-degree spin to the left may have added another 180-degree turn with both feet together on the beam. Again much depends on the gymnast's ingenuity and courage to try out new things.

(e) *Spin of 180 degrees on a bent leg*. This spin is one of the harder variety because the free leg is so close to the beam. The leg must be extended sideways so that a good hip flexion is possible. Once the flexion sideways is decreased the free leg touches the beam and overbalancing results.

Spin position. Squat on the beam sideways with the left leg extended and the right leg bent so that the seat touches the heel (wolf position). The left leg is now swung in an arc to the right and placed on the beam again. The right leg remains bent but turned out at the hip. The arms assist the spin because there is no speed to be gained from anywhere else. They swing to the left too, then to the right to enable the left leg to leave the beam. When the 180 degrees turn is proficient, instead of placing the left foot on the beam after 180 degrees it should be kept free above the beam to complete 360 degrees before touching the beam again. Progressions can even go as far as two and a half turns before touching the beam (Latynina Russia—World Champion).

COACHING FOR THIS SPIN: Very good hip flexion and strong quadriceps needed. The back must be kept straight so that the weight stays over the foot; keep on the ball of the foot—sinking to the heel results in immediate overbalance. Use the arms and don't be afraid to attack this spin—a half-hearted effort will surely result in a tumble. To check the spin the instep of the free foot should slap against the beam in an everted position. The arms and head also must stop dead to kill the momentum. The toes of the free leg may be regarded as a pencil in a pair of compasses, i.e. they should draw a circle or circles round the body.

Lunge position. This is used very often in a static position or as a stop from a spin. The feet are placed obliquely across the beam with a fairly wide space between. The front leg is flexed strongly and the rear leg extended. From this leg base many arm and trunk positions can be achieved. In the lunge there should be tremendous feeling of the legs working antagonistically—seesawing through bracing, not by movement.

All these spins, turns and balances have been arrived at by trial and error and by watching gymnasts of other countries who are far more superior in ability than ourselves. We have managed to import many of these ideas, adopt them into our coaching and adapt them for our methods of training. Naturally, every method will not suit each gymnast, therefore it is necessary for coach and teachers alike to use as much of this coaching as is practical for her groups of gymnasts to add to, select and throw out material and ideas which are not compatible to her scheme of work.

10. *More difficult agilities on the beam including those requiring a greater degree of mobility*

The majority of these movements are those which reach handstand or pass through, therefore coaching points for a handstand on the beam have been given once only. They apply to all the handstands, but slight differences appear depending on how the gymnast returns to the beam from it.

Handstand along the beam

Hand position: Both hands side by side, thumbs on the top of the beam, fingers spread down the side of the beam. A great deal of the weight is borne on the heel of the thumb. *Elbows:* These must be braced so that they lock. Because the base is so narrow it is necessary to have this locking for a steady foundation. *Shoulders:* The shoulders should be kept over the hands; a line should extend from hands, through the shoulders to the hip joint. *Trunk:* This should be in a state of tension, i.e. with the upper trunk lifted away from the lower. A straighter handstand should be the aim. The complete extension should pass through the legs. *Legs and feet:* These should be stretched with special emphasis on the knees and feet. The feet should again continue the line of the handstand though they may tend to be a little farther over than the shoulders.

All of these points go towards making a good handstand, but special mention must be given to the head position. The head should be held well back so that the gymnast may help to control the handstand by pressing it back to fight the position when learning.

(a) *Handstand to change legs.* This is a very useful method of approaching the handstand because a lesser or greater degree of 'kick up' can be used until confidence is gained. At first place the hands on the beam and kick off to land on the other leg, i.e. the legs change in the air to do a scissor. Gradually improve the kick up, but keep the arms very straight. If one elbow gives, the position will slip sideways. When a full handstand change legs is being attempted it is wise to have someone to stand by in case the handstand goes too far. Again the hips must be placed over the shoulders. Eventually kick into handstand from standing position and split the legs in changing them. Aim—to stay balanced while the legs change over, then to land back on the beam in complete balance.

(b) *Handstand with legs together.* Kick up to do a handstand just as though on the floor, but with the feeling of putting oneself into the air rather than kicking up violently. The handstand should be straight; too much hollowness will result in a slack handstand which is difficult to hold. From a well balanced handstand the roll can be added.

(c) *Handstand roll.* From the handstand (b) the tension is in the elbows; release this tension so that the shoulders lower to the beam as the head tucks in. Once the shoulders feel the beam, the grip on the top of the beam must be transferred underneath to provide the check as in the forward roll. The legs fold over the head so that the gymnast can see her knees. This again kills roll speed. A progression is a handstand roll to stand immediately, without altering the grip.

(d) On achieving a controlled handstand, leg pattern can be tried. Such is a stag position. The leading leg reaches as high as possible and the second leg bends at the knee. An oblique line can be made or a line passing through a higher position or one in which the leading leg is carried almost parallel to the beam. The second leg keeps the line too. To land on the beam the bent leg may stretch down to the beam or stretch up to join the other in handstand. From here a roll or a change of legs, depending on what is required. In handstands where the legs make a pattern other than the recognized straight handstand it is necessary for the hips and shoulders to become the fixed points on which the legs may work. Once the hip position is lost, either by falling or sinking back, the handstand is lost.

(e) *Lever handstand.* This demands a greater degree of strength because there is no kick-up to give impetus. The hands are placed on the beam and at the same time the legs are lifted both together up to handstand. The seat must pass well over the hands and shoulders in the first stage, but as the handstand is neared the seat and shoulders fall into line so that a normal handstand is maintained. Similarly a handstand lever-down to straddle-sit can be learned. From the handstand the shoulders are moved forward as though doing a chest roll but the hips and legs keep the handstand position. The elbows can either be kept straight, in which case the shoulders move farther forward still, or they can be bent, then the handstand lowers more or less on the spot. Those elbows flex, they do not relax. This is most important. This movement finishes in an astride position with the hips close to the hands and the legs wide enough to keep clear of the beam, otherwise burning through friction will result.

(f) *Cartwheel to handstand.* This has been discussed in the section on dismounts, so it is the final position with which we are primarily concerned.

Cartwheel to handstand and straddle down to stand on the beam. From the handstand position, facing sideways now, the hips and shoulders are very firmly fixed. They must stay in a static position because it is on the hips that the legs must work. The legs from handstand position widen into astride position, then the hips flex to allow the legs to lower. The trunk stays fixed very strongly, whilst the legs, extended and straight, are lowered to the beam. The last two feet down are the hardest, requiring much control. The fingers must maintain a firm grip too and the head help to control the body position. The feet are lowered on to the beam so that a sideways stance is produced with the legs wide outside the hands. Stand erect or turn into a lunge or lift off to hip-rest—numerous are the possibilities.

(g) *Straddle down to sit astride the beam.* This is a further progression of (f). The legs are kept wider and lowered to clear the beam. They then press forward so that in effect the knees are almost resting on the elbows; half-turn to either right or left to sit astride the beam.

(h) A further and more difficult progression on (f) is a handstand, straight-leg lever down to sit on the beam (legs together). From the handstand the same fixed postion of shoulders and hips is required, but a very great flexion at the hips is needed too to allow the feet to pass between the hands. Because the flexion is great the hips move forward over the shoulders, but the head should be pressed back very strongly. The hips must be kept up to allow space for the legs to pass through the hands. Again, the seat should be kept clear of the beam until the legs are stretched forward. Strong shoulders and hip flexors are a 'must' for this exercise.

(i) A simpler form of this movement is to bring one leg down to place between the hands to arrive in a mill sitting position. The free leg stays very high in the air and acts as a balance. At first the gymnast can aim to place the foot on the beam, then over it.

(j) *Cartwheel.* This must have a different approach on the beam compared with the floor because the element of fear arrives due to the narrowness and the height. It should be practised on the floor, on a line, on a form which is low, then on a low beam. It is a good idea to place a small piece of matting over the beam where the first foot will land. If the landing is fairly certain the mat can be removed. Shoulder support may be necessary too. The hands should be placed sideways just as they are on the floor, without a thumbgrip, one after the other. On the beam the handstand position can be passed through, but more often the wheel is cut down a little. The legs should move fairly slowly. The first leg should turn forward into the direction from which the gymnast has come. The foot should be everted to grip the beam. This foot and leg should act as a balancing leg, while the second leg is placed on the beam, well back from the first and also everted. This gives another grip. Immediately the trunk should be extended, though the legs will be in a lunge position. A simple form of cartwheel is that which lands in a crouch position, but once it is learned it is difficult to progress to a full cartwheel. The thumbgrip is now used in the wheel and as the first leg arrives on the beam the knee is bent into a crouch position and the first hand moved so that it grips alongside the second.

(k) *Splits on the beam.* Splits still maintains its popularity, probably because of the possibilities which arise from it as a movement of great suppleness. On the beam it is commonly executed sideways, but sometimes forwards. In splits on the beam the whole of both legs should be in contact with the beam—the back leg should be turned out at the hip. To arrive in splits different methods should be tried to find the easiest and most pleasing way, because a shuffle down into splits takes away any aesthetic value which it may have. This is a balance of a kind because the legs follow the line of the beam and there is nothing at either side on to which the gymnast can rely for help. Numerous positions can be used, just as the body may turn sideways, straight or twist at the shoulders. These twists in the shoulders lead to one or two very pleasing positions with the arms placed in opposition to the trunk. To alight on the beam from splits the gymnast has a wide selection of ways: (i) To lift off the back leg then the front and squat up. (ii) To lift off the rear leg and join it to the front. v sit up to stand. (iii) Lift off the rear leg, place the foot on the beam or the knee. (iv) Swing the front leg from the beam and join it to the back leg (the body falls forward on to the chest to allow this to happen). (v) Turns can be tried by lifting up on one hand and similarly turns can be used to get into splits.

If the gymnast has this necessary suppleness of limbs and trunk then her field of activities is far wider than one who is hampered by tight muscles. Muscle-suppling and limbering up is a book in itself, so very little mention has been made of it here, but most movements can be achieved by performing them rather than progressions. Splits should come very easily with continuous practice, but great care should be taken to see that the limbs are really warm first.

(l) *Backbend walkover on the beam.* This is an advanced mental movement, though not really difficult to do, but it takes a great deal of will-power to actually go for it. The first part of it is the hardest, i.e. the reach back.

COACHING: Stand on the beam (low), one foot in front of the other, as for a back walkover on the floor. Practise reaching up with trunk smoothly, then leaning back to sight the beam (a stand-by is necessary for this). From the reach-up and back the arms pass either overhead on to the beam or dislocate on to the beam (the latter simply means that the arms are turned in the shoulder joint to reach the same position as in the reach overhead). The dislocation is a quicker means of getting the hands on to the beam. The hands must be placed firmly in such a way that they can take body weight as the forward leg comes over the top. The elbows must be locked in this movement to prevent tipping to the side. The legs pass through a wide splits position slowly to allow the first leg to be placed on the beam with the foot everted. The second foot lands in the same way—slowly and turned out for grip. When the first foot is secure then the hands relax from the beam and the body becomes erect. A good backbend on the floor is necessary before attempting it on the beam. Stress should be laid on the stretch-up of the trunk, the controlled kick-over, the extension of the elbow and a steady landing. Stretch throughout.

A backbend to handstand is approached in the same way, but the first leg passes to handstand and the kicking leg then joins it. The hands are placed in the same way as the walkover, but the head must play an even bigger part—to press back to maintain the stand. When these bends can be done on a low beam (technical execution correct) then the beam should be raised. It will probably be necessary to use a little support again until the height of the apparatus has been felt. The support should be under the shoulder, but after the hands have touched the beam. It may be necessary to steady the movement and guide the first foot on to the beam. Bends such as these require much more practice than most movements because the first half of the movement is blind unless an extra-ordinary suppleness of the upper spine is developed.

(m) *Forward bend to stand*. Once again this is a movement requiring a great deal of determination and courage because the landing is blind. Walkovers should be prac-tised on a line of the floor until they are very accurate, then practised on a floor beam with the aid of helpers. The handstand is passed through and tremendous exten-sion of the trunk should be used to increase the hollow when walking over. The handstand 'musts' apply here as anywhere else and the walkover leg must be braced on landing, with the foot turned out across the beam. The beam actually crosses the instep. The pull-up of the trunk must be very rapid so that the beam can be sighted as soon as possible. If the suppleness at the upper spine is great enough it is possible for the gymnast to see the beam for the foot placing if the head is held well back. These advanced movements will be practised only by a gymnast in training, but nowadays more and more teachers are becoming interested in this kind of work and I feel they will be studied with great interest. Con-tinental books and pamphlets give a much greater degree of coaching because all the knowledge is at their finger-tips, plus a tradition in gymnastics up to which coach and gymnast may live.

Back somersault from the beam

It is necessary to refer to the agility section where back somersaults were coached in detail. As a finish from the beam they are quite common and give the gymnast a real feeling of leaving the beam before landing. Because the beam is high this does not mean that the somersault need not go up into the air. It must go well up and back to avoid the beam. The thrust is derived from the balls of the feet and the direction of thrust up through the knees into the hips. Immediately after the thrust the knees are pulled up quickly into tuck position for turnover. The stretch-out is just as quick, i.e. two movements up and tuck to turn over, then stretch out from the landing which is sighted. If the gymnast lands too far away from the beam the hips should be pushed a little forward on take-off; the somersault may be used as a finish from the side of the beam or from the ends.

This chapter on beam has been intended primarily for teachers who have not had the opportunity of being coached by British Gymnastic Association coaches. I have tried to correlate the ideas of educational gymnastics (freedom of the individual, experimentation, use of all parts of the body and, above all, selection by the individual after thinking around an agility) with the more definite form that advanced moves must necessarily take. Because of their difficulty, in many cases a formal movement has been offered plus the coaching and it is round this movement that freedom of choice can arise. Whilst many gymnasts love to play about with movements there are others who need greater guidance until the need for trying out is felt to be spontaneous. Nothing is more distressing than for a child to attempt to work out a sequence about which she has no ideas—nowhere to start, no means of finishing and what goes on in the middle. Her mind a complete blank. One formal movement can give incentive and then the satisfaction of achievement. From this achievement comes the urge to try more, and eventually she will be working out for herself sequences which will satisy both herself and her coach.

4

Asymmetric Bars

(OR HIGH AND LOW)

Asymmetric parallels is the name given to these bars because for women's work they are parallel but not of the same height. The top bar is approximately 7 ft. 6 in. and the low one 5 ft.

I have found these bars of very great use in my school because I have not got a gymnasium—therefore, no apparatus for swinging or heaving actions. After struggling for some time on home-made bars set up in the garden I eventually had some made by a shipyard. Now we have two sets in the school hall, which, together with the three beams and the school equipment, provide apparatus for a very wide range of movements and activities. The greatest handicap is the lack of floor space, but because of the nature of the hall many girls may work at once.

The bars are made so that either the top or bottom bar can be removed. This means that the lower bars may be used on their own or the top bars alone may be used for long swinging movements. It is possible for as many as four small children to use one set of bars at the same time, i.e. two on the top and two on the bottom. The lower bar is adjustable in height so that smaller children can reach, and they are adjustable in width for children who are small or short-limbed. This is where the parallels of the early twentieth century were not satisfactory. The higher bar is usually adjustable too, but because my bars are not exact in specification it was thought that it would be safer to have the top bar fixed at standard height. The wooden tops are oval in shape and they have a steel core to prevent snapping. These are imported from Germany because their equipment is still far superior to ours.

The aim in work on 'high and low' is to swing from one bar to another, circle round them, let go of one to catch the other, bounce over from one to another, keeping the movements going the whole time (bound flow is very apparent until the finish of an exercise when free flow may take over, especially from a long swinging movement). The bars are worked rather fast once ability is satisfactory, because this piece of apparatus does require a degree of strength and the faster the movements the greater the impetus, therefore less strength and energy are expended.

Exercises on high and low
The exercises have been grouped together under headings as follows:

1. Exercises demanding swinging and heaving and arching.
2. Exercises demanding springs from the feet.
3. Exercises demanding levering positions.
4. Exercises demanding the ability to let go of one bar to catch the other.
5. Mounts and dismounts.

Insufficient space remains to cover the field of bar work in anything like the detail required, but perhaps this is an advantage because it is on this piece of apparatus that we are so far behind other countries. Our ability to coach bars leaves a great deal to be desired. This is because we cannot ourselves get the coaching experience required in order to pass it on to active gymnasts.

1. *Swinging and heaving exercises*

These are the basis of all work on the bars; to be able to support body weight on the hands is the first stage, so to develop this a few exercises have been given.

(a) Hang on the top bar and swing forward and backwards by moving the legs to give forward momentum. Practise this movement using a leg whip rather than a swing. This whip should make the hands leave the bar for a split second. In order to mount the bar, the same movement is taken, but when the legs are whipped forward they lift over the bottom bar so that the body is in back rest. From here lift the legs through straddle sideways, join them together behind and repeat the whole movement. This not only strengthens the shoulders but the abdominals too.

(b) Hang on the top bar facing out, i.e. with back to the low bar. Use the same whip to lift the legs through the arms into half-inverted hang. Reach for the bottom bar

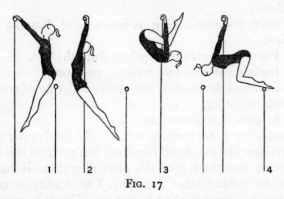

FIG. 17

with the top of the feet, then slide the bar up the shins past the knees until the body is as hollow as it can be with the arms in reverse. Release either hand, right, for example, and turn to the left. Place the free hand on the bar (lower) and finish sitting in riding seat with one hand on the top and one on the bottom. Another variation is to sit with the bar between the legs.

(c) Take the same movement again as far as inverted hang, then place both insteps or ankles on the bar. Turn in exactly the same way as in (b) but one foot will remain on the bar, the other will be free. The free leg should reach forward so that the gymnast stands on one foot, holding the top bar with one hand. (b) and (c) are methods of moving from the high bar to the low.

(d) *Backward circles and forward circles.* From the previous standing position on one foot, place both feet together on the low bar and place both hands on the high bar (fingers backwards); rest the hips on the top bar and allow the body to circle forward, feet leaving the bottom bar. For safety, ensure that the gymnast looks over the top of the bar after the circle to control the speed of the circle. This bends the arms, and the legs fall more slowly. The full hanging position will be with the hands in reverse, so a turn is necessary to face the low bar. Remove the right hand and turn in towards the bar, replacing the right hand. The position now is: long hanging with hands forward facing the lower bar.

(e) *Backward circles.* These are very useful movements because they strengthen arms and abdominals at the same time. Both forward and backward circles should be tried on the low bar first. To backward-circle place hands in a reverse grasp first. See that the hips are under the bar then kick up one leg leading. Join the other leg to it and circle over the bar backwards to hip-rest. The hands will finish in a position ready for a forward circle, i.e. with fingers pointing backwards. In the backward circle the hips must be thrown to the bar and the arms should be kept strong. The hips should not throw away from the bar. As the circle is being performed the head is put back, but not until the hips reach the bar. At first the movement will be rather piked, but as strength and timing develop, the position will hollow out. When the hips touch the bar the legs should remain still and the trunk lift into a balance position. The backward circle is also done with the hands in a forward grasp. This leaves the gymnast in a really ready position for many more movements. A backward circle over the top bar may be taken from sitting on the low bar. This demands speed of lift of the legs and a fixing of the arms to allow the hips to pass over the bar.

(f) *Lay off into a backward circle*. The hip-rest position is taken with hands (fingers forward) close to the hips. On the lay-off the shoulders go well forward as the hips lift away from the bar. This lay-off and return to the bar should be practised until falling forward or backward is conquered. When this is so, on returning to the bar the body circles backwards over the bar to finish in hip rest. Once again the legs remain high and the trunk lifts.

(g) *Swing from the top bar to long-hang and circle the bottom bar*. Position for start: Hip rest, fingers forward (thumbs round the bar at first), lay off gently from the top bar to long-hang and swing under the low bar with the legs. Fold at the hips so that the bar is in the fold. As the backward circle commences, release the top bar and grasp the bottom. The grip on the bottom bar must help to fix the trunk in order to loose the speed of the 'wrap'. This movement can be taught from a swing in to the low bar, without the lay-off the top at first. The pike position should be lost as soon as possible to enable the position to become a hollow wrap. A progression on this, too, is to circle the low bar without the hands (ready for movement to catch the top bar).

(h) *Short-arm position into a circle*. Start position: Sit on the low bar holding the top. Swing the legs through the hands and hook the knees on the bar. Release the hands from the bar and hang down by the knees, head back to see the low bar. Place both hands forward on the low

32 Free position for backward straddle   33 Backward straddle

34 Backward straddle from the rear

35   Handstand on
the asymmetric
bars

36   Forward seat
circle

bar. Push through so that the back is hollow, gently bend the arms and push the shoulders forward and at that time release the knees from the top bar. In this way the speed from the legs will cause a circle backwards. A little support may be necessary under the shoulders and hips because the movement will happen quickly in the initial stages, as the hips are inclined to drop away from the bar.

FIG. 18

(i) *Handstand to wrap or circle the low bar*. Sit on the low bar with hands on the top bar (fingers forward); swing the legs through the hands and bend the knees over the high bar. Having done this, hang down by the knees. Place both hands on the low bar with fingers facing the high bar (this is important). With a swift pull-and-push action the shoulders are placed over the hands and the elbows straightened. The foot is placed on the top bar in order to kick away to handstand balance, which is held momentarily. Gently the arms are bent and shoulders put forward so that a backward circle results. Finish is in a hip-rest position facing the high bar.

H

(j) *Heave-turn to circle the low bar*. Sit on the low bar, holding the high bar with both hands. Swing the legs forward and upwards and towards the top bar, lifting the hips up also. At the height of the lift heave and turn to either right or left when there is little weight on the hands. The turn brings the body in to the low bar to circle it backwards.

Preparation for this movement: (i) Take up the start and practise the heave with one or two supports to give the lift. The arms must be strong. (ii) Practise the turn to select the direction of turn from a swing in long hanging, i.e. not sitting on the bar. (iii) Now, with the aid of helpers, practise the heave and turn from sitting on the low bar with the helper initiating the turn at the highest point. The turn is aided by a movement at the hips and with the head, not with the shoulders. In the actual turn the heave should go higher than the bar (the hips remain high, therefore there is no weight on the hands). The swing in to the bar will be rather fast at first, so the swing to circle backwards should be well practised on the low bar. Finally the whole movement will continue into a backwards circle on the low bar. *Musts:* The arms must be kept strong and slightly flexed—the legs lifted high—the hips kept up to the bar—the turn made when there is little weight on the hands by the head and hips. The arms will be at full stretch after the turn is completed.

(k) A similar example of the heave position may be felt in the exercise when the legs are lifted clear of the low bar to bounce on it over to hip-rest on the top bar. Preparation for the bounce: (i) Hands in forward grasp on high bar— sitting position on low bar. Flex the elbows well to bring the shoulders up to the bar. Place one foot on the bottom bar to kick upwards and at the same time join the legs together. They bounce on to the low bar; the spring of the bar and bracing of the limbs causes the legs to shoot up and over the top bar. This bounce will not be successful until the knees are kept very straight to enable the bar to strike the back of the thighs. Any relaxation of the limbs will result in deadening of the bounce, which will cause pain. (ii) Hip-rest on top bar—forward circle, keep the hips very high and allow only the legs to come down to bounce on the bar. The ideal position should be flat and not piked at all.

Final movement: From long hanging on the top bar facing the low bar. Swing in to the low bar, as though going to circle it, but whip the legs backwards. Next lift the legs up forward and very high into a heaving position, then flatten the body so that the bounce is very controlled. This is where the pike position should be avoided because if the hips drop there is no depth for the bounce. Once the legs have bounced over the bar they should remain still and high, while the trunk and head lift up to make the position static.

FIG. 19

(1) *Mill circles forward and backwards.* A rule to remember when learning mill circles is: When circling forward the thumbs should be forward, when circling backwards the thumbs should be backwards, i.e. pointing in the direction of the circle. The aim for circles is to maintain the starting position throughout and finish in the same position. *Backward circles:* Most gymnasts find these easier

than forwards, so they have been taken first. Start: Sit astride the bar with either right or left leg forward. Left leg for example. Extend both legs into a wide astride and sit up very straight. The hands are placed on the bar beside the hips with the fingers facing forward. From this position lift clean of the bar and place it across the back of the left thigh (the body rotates about this point). Fall backwards, maintaining the body position with a slight arch in the back and by whipping the back leg (right) towards the left. The hands slide round the bar to finish on the top in the same grasp. Care must be taken to keep the body and legs facing forwards, otherwise a side circle will result. Gradually the whip in of the leg will be diminished and the whole movement will become smoother. The thumbs round the bar play an important part in the checking of a circle together with the trunk position.

Once again extension throughout is the key-note. *Forward circles:* These are exactly backward mill circles done in reverse. The movement travels forward round the bar, therefore the thumbs are placed forward. The body is lifted so that the weight is placed on to the back leg as the gymnast feels 'walking over the bar'. The body should remain erect, i.e. maintain the starting position all the way through. A very proficient gymnast will probably not use thumbs round the bar because the ability to stop will be so well timed that her next movement will follow straight on.

(m) *Seat circles forward.* From sitting, legs extended together on the low bar, hands alongside the hips, thumbs forward in the direction of the circle. Erect position of trunk. Lift the seat clear of the bar and at the same time the trunk folds forward on the legs, nose to knees. This position is maintained until the rise above the bar when the legs are extended downwards, i.e. the fold opens out. It is a mistake to open out too soon because this results in hollowing the back over the bar instead of circling. The finish again should be as the start. When this movement is being performed with the high bar behind, the gymnast can open out to catch the top bar. It is possible to sight the bar on the way up from the circle. The bar should remain high at the back of the thighs, not be pulled into the small of the back. This is what happens when the body hollows over the bar.

(n) *Seat circles backwards*. This is taken exactly in reverse of the forward seat circle, but more impetus backwards is used. The bar must remain at the back of the thighs until the circle is completed. The circle may be simplified by bending the knees on the last part of the circle. This serves to shorten the circle. Once back on top of the bar the legs must extend again and press down. This is a useful movement to precede the hock swing.

2. *Springs from the feet*

Springs may be attempted as soon as the gymnast looks at home on the bars. Many of the simple dismounts are simply jumps from the bottom bar over the top bar. For this purpose the bottom bar may be used as the top and a box in sections placed as the lower bar. If both bars are adjustable then they can be lowered to suit the ability of the class. When progression has been made to mounts over the top bar, if the top bar is fixed then the bars can be moved to a platform to counteract the height from the top bar. Gradually sufficient confidence will be given so that dismounts can be done on the bars at normal height.

(a) *Crouch jumps over the top bar*. Place both hands on the bar and spring from the bottom bar over sideways to land in a good position on the floor. The knees tuck up and the hips lift clear of the bar. The weight must be borne on the hands. When springing over to the right the left hand may be reversed and vice versa.

(b) *Flank vault over*. Same hand position and spring, but

the knees remain straight throughout and the legs extended sideways from the hips so that the side of the trunk passes over the top bar. Landing is in a forward position. The hands do not remain on the bar for any length of time.

(c) *Straddle* (leapfrog over). It is very important that this should be well practised at a low height in order to get the legs into a wide enough position to clear the bar because seat height is not required. Both hands are placed on the top bar as the feet spring upwards and the legs straddle wide to clear the bar. Once over, the trunk is extended to prevent landing on all fours. The head must be kept back. During the extension of the trunk the legs should be snapped together to prepare for landing. A good smooth landing surface is needed for these dismounts because of the height. The feet and ankles should take most of the landing weight and little by the knees.

(d) *A spring from one foot.* This is taken sideways from the bottom bar over the top to sit. Stand with left hand holding the bar, swing up the left leg and spring from the right foot over the top bar, legs extended. The left remains extended but the right bent at the knee. As soon as the sitting position is felt, the right hand grasps the bar alongside the right leg. Sit up in a good position from here, turn to hip-rest on the top bar and a forward circle over the top bar may be executed to sit in riding seat on the low bar.

(e) *Straddle over to sit on the top.* This is a similar movement to the clear straddle, but in this much greater control is needed. The spring is from the feet as the hands grasp the bar, but the seat is not pushed forward to clear the bar, but kept above it. The legs straddle round and rest on the elbows to keep the seat clear. The head and trunk must be kept in line, and once the head drops the straddle falls forward. The knees must be kept braced to maintain the position, and the elbows too. From this position the trunk may fall back and the legs straddling wider clear the top bar. The body is then in long hanging, facing away from the low bar. It is not possible to explain the numerous ways in which these movements may be finished, but a great deal of satisfaction will be had by coach and gymnast alike to determine just how many ways can be found.

(f) *Jump feet through to sit*. This demands an immediate extension of the legs and trunk to form a right angle at the hips once the bent legs have passed between the hands. The start of the movement is the same as in the straddle, i.e. the spring and hand position. Once the right angle is achieved, the seat should be placed on the bar and the legs lowered so that the position becomes back rest. Turn over to front rest and progress from there.

(g) Once straddle movements are confident they may be tried backwards, i.e. a jump backwards over the top bar, placing the hands on afterwards. This may be practised from a box top over the low bar to get the feeling of jumping first, then putting the hands on the bar. To progress to the top bar: Stand on the low bar with fingers resting on the top bar back to the top bar too. Spring upwards and backwards, releasing the hands to allow the legs to straddle, then catch again between the legs. The feet and legs must remain extended, otherwise the heels will not clear the bar. Once the catch is made, the legs must be brought together into long position. The feeling of the back straddle should be approached gently. Some gymnasts will 'go' for it immediately, but for those who are a little nervous, but who wish to try, they should progress through springing back to sit in straddle; spring back and up a little farther each time until the bar is cleared. When the gymnast feels very confident of the catch she may try a 'free' back straddle, i.e. one in which the hands are placed on the bar only after the jump. This movement is prepared for in the way of a diver doing a back dive. Both arms are extended forward in line with the shoulders, while the balance is made on the low bar by the balls of the feet. The arms assist the upward spring of the body to straddle backwards over the bar. Once the gymnast decides to do this movement there should be no hesitation or turning of the head because this will result in an uneven straddle or an unsuccessful catch.

(h) *Standing by for straddles* (forward and backward). Methods which I have found useful: Forward straddle to sit and over. Stand on a high box behind the low bar and grip the back of the suit of the gymnast. (Or if necessary put a belt round to give more grip.) This way gives no support but assists in confidence, also the stand-in is out of the way of the straddling legs. Gradually less and less grip is used until the forward straddle is achieved alone. It is a good plan to have someone standing by on the floor in case the straddle is rather violent. When straddling over to clear, the coach may adopt the same method but standing on the bar at one side. If this is used great care must be taken to see that there is room for the foot to clear on that side. *Standing in for the back straddle:* A high buck or box should be placed behind the high bar sufficiently far away to allow the gymnast to spring back. At first the sides of the gymnast are held while she is jumping back to sit on the bar. When she intends to jump clear, the buck should be moved out a little. Then the first part, i.e. the jump, is made alone, the coach coming in when the hands catch the bar again. This is very useful just in case the hands do not catch the bar again. Sufficient grip is maintained to control the straddle. Finally the back is removed, the complete action takes place, but until it is very accurate the coach should be behind for this straddle. It may be found necessary to build confidence for this for several weeks, and even after this is conquered it may be lost again. Practice with coaching will soon bring it back into the gymnast's routine.

(i) *Jump to forward straddle, heave-turn to circle the low bar.*
This is the jump to forward straddle given earlier in this
section. From the straddle there follows a drop back
between the two bars, but the hips must remain high
above the bar as the legs straddle out while in this very
high position. A heave turn is made closing the legs
together so that the body swings in to the low bar for a
backward circle. The main coaching point for this
movement is to link the heave turn with the straddle
without allowing the hips to drop.

(j) Similarly a jump to straddle, the feet very wide
on to the top bar, may be used—the rest of the movement
remains the same.

(k) The straddle position with feet on the bar facing
outwards may be taken from hip-rest position. This gives
another variety.

(l) *Dislocation movements.* The word dislocation con-
jures up the feeling that these movements will hurt. It
does not, in fact, when it is done properly with correct
training. Once again it is necessary to 'go' for it. Half-
hearted attempts will not succeed, especially in this.
Preparation: (i) Stand with the back to low bar and place
the hands fairly wide by lifting the arms up and backwards.
The fingers point backwards (back-crawl reach position
again). From here sink at the knees, lower the shoulders
and allow the head to pass under the bar. Stand up
between the two bars. The shoulders, or rather the head
of the humerus, is taken forwards down and back upwards, i.e. circling in the joint. This is really what the
movement is, not a true dislocation. The arms should
gradually be narrowed a little so that the feeling of
circling in the joint is increased. The head moves forwards too—it follows the circling action of the shoulders.
(ii) Stand on a box top with hands placed in dislocation
grasp. Bend the knees to a squat position. Now push the
seat up between the arms by folding at the hips, head

well down to the knees. Attempt the dislocation by swinging in the inverted position under the bar to shoot the legs high behind. At this point there is no weight on the hands and shoulders, so the dislocation is made without effort or hurt. Two supports must be prepared to take the weight as it falls because the movement has been prepared near to the floor. It is invaluable to learn to dislocate on the rings because the movement is so much easier due to the pliable nature of the rings. Dislocation practice from the box top should be attempted many times so that the gymnast does the movement alone—the only support coming in to stop the drop after the layout. The head folds to the knees for the first part of the dislocation. Once the movement is made, the head is thrown back; this helps the actual dislocation. It may be found easier to allow the hands to slide apart a little. This means that a very high shoot of the legs can be achieved. *The actual dislocation:* Stand on the low bar, back to the high bar, with hands in dislocation grip. Repeat the whole of the second preparation, but on the two bars instead of the box top. It is wise to have stand-ins raised from the floor to enable more body weight to be taken for the first few attempts. The higher the shoot of the legs, the faster will be the swing in to the low bar, but the swing should be with control, trunk extended.

(m) *Dislocations from sitting on the top bar.* Only the starting position of this differs—sit on the top bar, legs extended forward, hands placed wide in disclocation grasp. Lift the seat clear of the bar and fold at the hips, head down on to the knees. The forward swing passes under the bar and the same dislocation is made as in (l).

(n) Similarly, dislocation can be made from sitting on the low bar, hands on the high bar in 'L' grasp (dislocation grasp). The legs are passed between the hands very swiftly to shoot backwards and upwards. There is very little swing for this movement, so the timing must be even more accurate.

3. *Levering position—squats*

These may be done on either the top or the bottom bar. In each of the following movements the shoulders are fixed to allow the trunk and legs to lever.

(a) *One-leg squat.* This is done from front-leaning rest on the low bar with hands placed forward (thumbs round the bar); for safety. The shoulders are brought well forward over the hands and the head kept in line. Both legs are thrown backwards and upwards from the bar, then at the height of the throw one leg is brought back and over the bar between the hands to sit with one leg forward and one leg backward in an extended position. The elbows must remain straight and the hips high until the foot has passed between the hands. This may be practised with both legs. The fingers must grip the bar well to control the movement.

(b) *Squat both feet on bent legs.* This is very similar to (a) except that the legs work symmetrically and bend together to allow the feet to rest on the bar (on the balls of the feet). The throw-away is the same, but the legs bend to accommodate the squat position. As the squat nears perfection it will be found that the 'lay off' the bar decreases and the shoulders do more work.

(c) *Squat over to sit.* Once again this is approached like (b), but the feet pass over the bar. The seat should remain clear, the legs extended forward, the elbows straight and fingers gripping. When this is achieved the seat should rest on the bar and the legs press downwards.

(d) *Straddle to stand.* From hip-rest position, the shoulders well forward and head up (but not back), thrown back and up from the bar with the hips at highest straddle, the legs wide to place the feet on the bar outside the hands. The hands and head play a great part in maintaining the straddle.

(e) Progressing from this is the *straddle to release hands*. The movement is exactly the same, but done with more determination, because when the legs straddle round, the hands are replaced outside the legs so that the finished position is that of a squat over to sit. The action produces a little bounce on the bar, which drops the gymnast back to half-inverted hang. On the straddle the bar comes across the back of the knees, so they should be braced really hard to stop bending.

(f) *Straight-leg squat to stand and to sit*. This demands a very good lay-off from hip rest with the shoulders well forward. The hips must lift very high to allow a pike which brings the feet to the bar, legs straight and together. The thumbs round the bar help to check the movement, although the aim is not to stay in a position but to press directly into another. Squat over to sit. This means that the hips must lift even higher to allow the feet to pass through the hands. The arms must be very strongly controlled to enable back-leaning rest to follow. Once the feet are through, they should press down while the trunk presses back.

All of these squats, once proficient on the low bar, can be introduced on the top bar. If they are done facing the low bar it is easy to stand in simply by taking the left arm of the gymnast (coach on the left standing on low bar) to steady her for the first few attempts. If the gymnast has difficulty in getting a good lay-off help may be given too by assisting on the lift. This should not be given too often or too long because the help gives the wrong sense of achievement. Standing in should be more for safety than assisting.

(g) *Squat, both feet on the low bar, with one hand on the top bar and one on the bottom*. This movement requires a slightly different technique because of the asymmetry of the movement. The hand on the top bar must pull downwards after the lay-off—this is to lift the hips to get them high enough to allow the feet to alight on the low bar. If this pull is not apparent the movement turns into an uncontrolled flank vault.

The hand on the low bar acts as the fixed point as in all squats. The weight gives forwards over the hand, but in this case the weight not only goes forward but to the side, e.g. hip rest on the low bar, right hand to the top (the pulling hand), the left on the low bar to bear the weight forwards and to the left. This, once learned, is a safe movement because one hand is always holding the bar, but care should be taken to see that it is learned on both sides and that it is not taught until a true squat is very confident. Asymmetric movements often tend to twist unless the gymnast has been well prepared to tackle such movements.

(h) *Squat over the top bar to stand on the low bar.* This may be taught as soon as the squat-on (both feet together) and the squat-over to sit is well controlled. For this movement very little hip lift is necessary, but a good shoulder lever is required. The squat-over is slower, then as the feet pass over the bar the legs extend in order to stand on the low bar. The hands remain on the top bar.

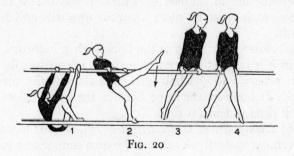

FIG. 20

4. Movements which demand the ability to let go of one bar to catch the other

(a) *Hock swing*. This is a circle of the low bar by the back of the knees to catch the top bar with the hands.

START: Sit on the low bar facing the high bar with knees bent (bar in the crease), hands holding the top bar for balance. Do not sit too low on the bar.

ACTION: Throw backwards away from the high bar with the arms extended above the head. Keep the knees bent to produce a pivoting point. The arms make as large a circle as possible as the trunk passes beneath the low bar. The impetus causes the trunk to swing up towards the top bar and, because the arms are above the head, they will catch the top bar. Arms and hands in a back-crawl position to catch the top (dislocation grasp).

FINISH: Long hanging from the top bar facing away from the low bar, the knees having released their grip on the low bar. The 'catch' is blind, therefore this movement must be done many times to produce the accurate timing needed.

This hock swing of above, once proficient, can be done on knees which produce a right angle instead of 45 degrees. This makes for an easier hock, as it doesn't scrape the back of the knees so much. The hock can also be practised from a starting position with hands on the low bar. The difference lies in the fact that there is less height in the throw, so it must be more vigorous upwards and backwards.

An easier hock swing is the hock with a half-turn, but again it is better to learn a movement symmetrically first then progress to the half-turn even though the turn is easier. It takes longer to go back to the hock dislocation catch than to learn it first.

(b) *Hock half-turn to either right or left*. This is the same movement basically as (a), but the turn commences just as the body starts to come up towards the top bar. It is a good plan to have the gymnast swinging by the knees, then half turning to choose the most natural side. Once the side is chosen then the full movement can be tried. The turn means that the gymnast catches the top bar, facing it with hands in the easy forward grasp. The knees stay bent until the catch has been made. At first there may be difficulty in catching with both hands, but this will come with practice and confidence.

Standing by for hock swings. These are movements which should not be attempted without actual manual holding by the stand-in. This is because the knees do not always stay bent when they should so that the body flies away from the bar. The supports should stand, one on each side of the bar. Pass the near hand under the bar to grip the waist of the gymnast, while the other hand ensures a bent-knee position. The right hand holds the feet to keep the knee-bent position secure. From here the gymnast makes the swing and even if the catch is not made, or the knees straightened, the gymnast is in full control. The other support catches in the same way. When a half-turn is put into action one support is adequate—the other actually would be in the way for the turn. If the turn is to the left the coach should stand in on the left to avoid the swinging arms.

(c) *Stand on the low bar facing the top drop back to catch the top.* This movement requires plenty of practice to develop the split-second timing. It can be done from strength standing or from feet together. Whichever way demands the same action but the straddle is easier because the feet can be kept on the bar in a wide position if they are everted a little.

Drop back with feet together.

START: Stand on the low bar feet together, knees straight, toes gripping the bar, hands on the top bar for balance.
ACTION: Both hands are placed on the low bar, one

either side of each foot (the thumbs remain alongside the fingers for extra grip. *N.B.* Wrong thumbgrip in photo). The body is allowed to fall backwards (trunk and legs piked). The gymnast must think consciously of pressing down on the bar with the feet and pulling up towards the shoulders with the hands, i.e. hands and feet work antagonistically (knees must remain extended). The feet stay on the bar as long as possible, then, when the top bar is sighted, the grip on the low bar is released to catch the top. The legs should be kept in a high forward lift until the hands grasp the top bar.

FINISH: Long hanging, facing away from the low bar. Tension must be felt in the body throughout the whole of the action; this movement can be led up to by doing the first part, but instead of catching the top a heave swing forward is used as a finish. Gradually, by keeping the feet on the bar longer and longer, they will be high enough to develop the catch.

Standing in. Two supports, one on each side. The drop back will be done by the gymnast alone and once the body is under the bar the supports come in with the near hand under the small of the back and the other under the thigh. To give confidence on the drop back the rear hand may be placed on the foot with a little pressure, then changed under the back.

A progression of this is to catch with a half-turn. The whole movement is the same until just before the catch. At this point (if the turn is to the left) the left hand catches in a forward grasp while the right catches in a forward grasp but facing the other way, i.e. the right hand will have the fingers pointing to the low bar and the left hand the fingers pointing away from it. This is because of the turn. The legs do very little in the turn except follow the hips round to the left.

FINISH: Long hanging facing the low bar, left hand in reverse grasp, right hand in forward grasp.

37 Front-leaning rest on top bar in preparation for squats

38 Bent-leg squat over the top bar

39 Straight-leg squat over the top bar

40 Back-leaning rest

When the drop back is done from straddle stand the legs must be snapped together before the catch of the top bar.

(d) *Lay off the top bar to circle the lower bar and catch the top in dislocation grip.* This movement requires a great deal of determination and timing for the catch, though if bars are used which have a good whip the catch is very much easier.

START: Hip-rest on the top bar.

ACTION: Lay off into a good but controlled swing to circle the lower bar in a hollow position. Very early in the wrap the trunk must be extended farther so that the body springs away from the low bar, i.e. from just above the hips. The spring must travel upwards and backwards so that the extended arms help the catch which is made in dislocation grasp. The body must be very well braced to make the spring from the bar, otherwise the trunk will flop forward over the low bar. It is not necessary to use a great deal of speed for this movement if the timing is correct. The spring must come early after the wrap or no backward whip will be felt. This same movement can be used up to the circle of the low bar, but a half-turn right or left is used to catch the top bar. Again this is easier because it is a sighted catch, but the hips must stay on the bar to give the spring. Circling of the bottom bar with the trunk in a relaxed position will not produce the whip from the bar to enable the grasp to be made on the high bar.

There are many other movements on bars in which the gymnast may leave one bar to catch another, but as yet in England the coaching of these movements is very much trial and error. Until this is remedied films and Continental books must remain our main help. One day perhaps we may have a coaching school with all the facilities to be gained by such a scheme.

I

5. *Mounts and Dismounts*

(a) Backward circles. These have been taken in Section 1.

(b) Start from long-hanging position on high bar.

(c) Start by placing one hand on the high bar, one on the low and standing sideways between the bars. Swing the legs forward and lift them over the low bar into riding seat. The top hand pulls and the bottom hand pushes to enable the seat to arrive above the bar.

(d) Squat on to the low bar with a run. Take off from a beating board and place both hands on the low bar. Immediately squat the feet between the hands, stand.

(e) Run and spring up, placing both hands on the low bar to arrive in short-arm position with the legs extended against the top bar. Place one foot on the bar (top) and push away to circle the bottom bar backwards. The shoulders are pushed forward so that the wrap is at hip level.

(f) *Long underswing to squat one leg through*. Long underswings: These take a great deal of practice before they are good enough to enable the gymnast to arrive at top of the bar. *Preparation:* (i) Kneel under the low bar with toes turned up in order to push, hands in forward grasp on low bar. From kneeling, push the body weight backwards, seat leading so that the feet leave the ground last. This produces a swing forward in pike position, requires strong quadriceps and the ability to fix the abdominals. The whole movement comprises a push back, swing forward and swing back until able to stand. (ii) Progress from standing so that the body is arm's length away from the bar. Bend the knees so that the body gives forward, then push from the feet, backwards, seat leading into the same underswing.

This movement is a swing not a spring, i.e. the gymnast must not spring forward into it. The arms must be kept at full extension, otherwise the body will drop. Practise this movement, getting the seat higher and farther back to increase the swing, but do not jump into it forwards. Gradually, as timing and ability increase, a gentle layout on the forward spring can be developed. From this it is possible to work the legs and trunk so that continuous underswings are performed. This is excellent for strengthening the muscles. (iii) The whole movement:

START: Stand back from the bar about a yard with the arms outstretched. Swing the arms backwards then forwards to grasp the bar. At the same time the seat is pushed back and high so that the feet clear the floor. Swing under the bar in this piked position but flatten at the end of the swing (do not hollow). From this flat position the legs fold on the trunk and the leg is passed extended between the hands. The swing forward should not be cut short in an effort to pass the leg through. This does not help in the arriving on top of the low bar. The complete movement pattern is: Push back, swing forward, swing back, one leg through, swing forward and rise above the bar to finish in mill sitting position. It is quite easy to rise above the bar with a bent leg, but if the swing is correct a straight leg will result, together with the whip downwards of the free leg.

FIG. 21

(g) *Long underswing to pass both legs through.* This is the same movement as (f), but the swing must have more force, especially after the fold at the hips. Both legs pass between the hands so that a really good pike is shown. Movement pattern—push back, to clear the feet, seat high and back, swing forward, flatten, lift the legs between the hands on backward swing (don't cut it short in the effort to rise above the bar) to finish sitting on the bar in back rest. The legs move in a high position because of the last part of the swing, therefore, once arriving above the whole bar, they should press down to back-rest.

(h) *Long underswing to straddle up.* This is a progression on (g). All the coaching applies up to the end of the forward swing, but in the straddle the legs pass astride the hands. The gymnast arrives on the bar with hands between the legs in a narrow straddle.

(i) *Long underswing to upstart.* Once again the same preparations are used for the swing but after the forward swing the legs are brought to the bar (not passed between the hands). The thighs act as a fixed point in the back swing around which the grasp of the hands can be shifted over the top of the bar, but the arms must be kept straight. As the grasp is moved, the legs beat down, which causes the body to rise above the bar to hip-rest. The handgrasp must be moved very rapidly and the arm strength maintained.

(j) *World Games set start on bars.* Stand with back to the low bar, facing away from high bar, and place both hands on the bar in 'L' grasp (the feet should be under the shoulders). Vigorously spring the seat up between the hands so that it rises above the bar; fold at the hips nose to knees and from here the movement is a forward-seat circle, but because of lack of forward momentum the arms must be used strongly. The pike position should be maintained because this increases the speed. Once the body opens out, speed is lost and hollowing over the bar results. The hands move round the bars, they do not release at all. This movement can be altered slightly so that instead of completing the movement in sitting position on the bar, with hands alongside, the circle can be opened out to catch the top bar with two hands.

Some other dismounts

(a) From hip rest on the top bar place both hands on the low bar, forward grip. At the same time throw away from the bar (top) by lifting the hips clear. A handstand is now shown on the low bar. Overthrow to land on the floor. Very little push in this is needed because of the height of the bar.

(b) *Handstand quarter-turn* (coaching for such a handstand given on beam). The same points apply but landing is easier from the bar because of 5 ft. as opposed to 3 ft. 11 in.

(c) *Handstand, squat the feet through* (straight leg and bent leg). The only small difference here is that the handstand is held on the bar, which may cause greater difficulty than on the flat surface of the beam, and that a certain amount of whip must be allowed for from the bar.

(d) *Handstand on the top bar.* This is a lever handstand, using a spring from the feet on the lower bar to initiate the lever. The spring transfers the weight from the feet over the shoulders and hands so that the hips are over the shoulders. The arms must be kept straight, otherwise the movement becomes a press-up. From this position the legs straddle wide and up to a handstand. The balance should be held long enough to show a good position before squatting the feet through the hands or making a quarter-turn to finish. The handstand should be prepared for in an easy stage and at a level so that stand-ins may be used. For this method again a box top can be used as the low bar and the low bar as the top bar. Springing up to the lever handstand can be practised with help on both sides (support under the shoulders at first, then give a little help to the straddling legs). If the shoulders and hips are put well over to start the movement the straddle will follow easily. Gradually the low bar can be raised and the box accordingly, so that the handstand is being executed at almost correct height. From here it is an easy step to progress to the two bars at regulation height. The lever handstand should be a good one on the floor before attempting on the bars.

Space will not allow of further coaching on movements on the bars, so a list of exercises follows.

For B.A.G.A. personnel the interpretation of these will be easy, but it is recommended that any teachers wishing to advance in gymnastics of this kind should attend coaching courses organized by the Gymnastic Association in order to become familiar with the technical terms given to many movements.

1. Hock swing from bottom bar as a finish.
2. Hock swing from top bar as a finish.
3. Rear vault over top bar as a finish.
4. Rear vault with half-turn.
5. Straddle over top bar with half-turn.
6. Squat over, feet between hands to land on the ground.
7. Hecht off to finish facing forward.
8. Hecht with half-turn to finish sideways.
9. Handstand wheel-out finish.
10. Heave finish over low bar from the high.
11. Short-arm overthrow from top bar.
12. Short-arm overthrow from low bar.
13. Straddle finish over top and bottom bars to land.
14. Drop back into inverted hand—on the back swing pull up and straddle out to finish.
15. Drop back into inverted hang—on the back swing pull up and release one hand, to land sideways.

Most of the movements given in this chapter have been called by their technical names, but in addition each move-

Fig. 22

ment has been explained. So often complaints are made
that set work cannot be understood by those setting out
to coach because of the incomprehensibility of the terms.
This, I hope, has been overcome here, but, of course, some
movements are difficult to explain without using their
technical names.

5

Vaulting

The horse is one of the pieces of apparatus included in the Olympic four, therefore it plays a great part in gymnastics as a whole. Vaulting is the part of a gym lesson which usually causes a cry of 'Good, its vaulting now!' This because excitement and satisfaction are closely linked together when a feat of courage is demanded. It should not be forgotten, though, that vaulting may cause a great deal of heartbreak to a nervous gymnast. Such a gymnast should not be forced into vaulting but left to experiment on apparatus. Perhaps she will never be able to do more that a few simple vaults, but she will not leave school only to say 'I was no good at gym and hated it'. On the other hand, with confidence in the coach a timid performer will have a try and probably surprise herself at her own capabilities. So much depends on the ability and temperament of the individual. If this is considered, and a wide choice of activities given, every gymnast should get some satisfaction from clearing an obstacle whether she vaults or not.

A different approach to vaulting is arising now in England. A style is being adopted, one which has been set by Ute Starke of Eastern Germany who won the Gold Medal in the European Cup in Leipzig in 1961. This changing trend was apparent in the Olympic Games in 1960, but the European Cup brought the standard to the fore. The vaulting technique is now similar to that used by men in vaults over the long horse, but for women's work the broad horse only is used. As a result, the length of the horse is omitted, but the actual length remains because the board is placed six or seven feet away from the aparatus. The board used is a Reuther board, one which has very little spring, so the gymnast must develop her own. The approach is a fast but controlled run of ten to sixteen steps before the gymnast places two feet on the board for a flight which must carry her over the gap and

APPROACH AND RUN UP FOR CHAMPIONSHIP VAULT

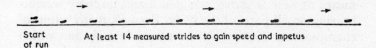

Start
of run   At least 14 measured strides to gain speed and impetus

PATH OF FLIGHT OVER HORSE

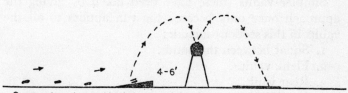

4 - 6'

Coast on last three strides before take off

Fig. 23

above the horse. A very great flight is needed to arrive on top of the horse, and if the speed is correct a further flight off the horse is the result. In other words, the hand-stand drop-off is out of date. This has been realized abroad for a long time, but it is not until quite recently that we have started to adopt this style of vaulting in Britain. A handicap immediately presents itself. There are about four or five Reuther boards in the whole of Britain, so our efforts to keep up with the counterparts abroad fall down at once. One club in Leipzig, for example, would have five boards, the number for the country running into hundreds. Greater attention is being given in this chapter to vaults of the ten tariff because the lower tariff vaults are used in schools quite often, perhaps not with a name attached but nevertheless they are being put into action. *The Proficiency Book of Gymnastic Tests* gives a reasonably full tariff table of vaults, also the suggested vaults for third-, second- and first-class awards.

Before a child learns to vault she must become familiar with the apparatus or obstacle placed in her path. Methods of arriving on, jumping off and over provide the necessary means as well as giving confidence and teaching weight-bearing on all parts of the body. Even so, many vaults of championship pattern can be woven into themes which demand that weight be borne on the hands only. This determines whether a vault is a vault or not, i.e. the hand only may be placed on the apparatus.

Simpler vaults (these have been taken by giving the approach once only because the run applies to all the vaults in this section) include:

1. Squat between the hands.
2. Flank vault.
3. Rear vault.
4. Straddle (with and without turn).
5. Short-arm overthrow.

Approach. The run-up for vaults 1–5 should be short, controlled but with springy, non-hesitant steps. The gymnast will soon determine with which foot she prefers to start and which foot will be the last to leave the floor. For the simpler vaults the gymnast should develop the ability to run freely, i.e. with no choice of starting foot but simply to regard the horse as an obstacle. It is for convenience and ease that movements are given technical names and the names themselves partly describe the vault. For example, squat between the hands suggests the tuck of the knees, straddle determines a leapfrog position and rear gives the idea of the seat passing over the horse.

1. *Squat between the hands*

The approach run is as given. The board right from the start should not be placed very close to the horse because this directs the spring too far forward instead of upward. A small flight should be made from the feet on to the hands —the latter may be slapped on to the horse to give quick release. The feet after beating are brought up quickly, knees bent, then extended to land on the mat. The gymnast should be encouraged to use spring right from the start—to make a determined vault rather than just going over any way. Style is most important, and in vaulting especially the head position plays a great part in controlling the vault. It acts as a break and the eyes assist landing by sighting something for the finish. It cannot be said too often that extension of the trunk is needed in each and every vault on landing. This enables a 'stop' to be produced, because in vaulting as a pure vault movements forward or backwards are not allowed without penalization. (This year under F.I.G. rules one step may be made in the direction of the vault without penalization, but naturally a vault which has a landing without a fraction of a movement calls for a higher mark.)

The landing. An easy, controlled landing is what is required, but with complete extension and no rebounds. The arms control the movement naturally and when they are brought to the sides the vault is considered completed. These rules for vaulting apply only to championships, but it is necessary to train right from the start. Let me make it quite clear that I am talking about vaults as such, not as vaulting movements placed in a sequence of work which may demand continuity, i.e. a vaulting movement, roll, spring and leap on to a piece of further equipment. I am dealing with vaults purely as a separate part of the Olympic sport.

2. *Flank Vault*

The legs pass to one side of the horse in an extended line, so that the side or the flank of the gymnast is nearest to the horse. A line is sought from the head through the shoulder, hips and knees and toes, i.e. there should be no bending of the knees or piking at the hips. The spring from the feet on to the hands, placed forward, takes the gymnast above the horse. The weight is taken on one arm, shoulder over the hand, and the other hand moved to lie along the side of the gymnast, e.g. weight on one arm, legs to the right, right arm along the right side. The legs pass clear of the horse, gaining as much height as is possible without flexing at the hips. This position is maintained for the landing so that the finish is with the back to the horse, hands by the sides, trunk erect. The gymnast can consider herself the pendulum of a clock—swing up in a flat position above the horse and swing down the other side to land. The body position remains the same.

3. *Rear vault*

This vault is determined by the fact that the seat passes nearest to the horse. The hands are placed forward on the horse from a forward run with the body facing forward too. Immediately the feet spring from the board the hips turn so that the body achieves a 'V' position facing the side. (Seat near horse, head and shoulders back, feet and legs extended, knees near the nose.) Assuming that the vault is executed to the right, the right hand is removed from the horse and placed behind on the horse when the body has passed over it. This means that the left arm is free and swings out to the side on the landing which is sideways right side to the horse. Vaults should be executed on both right and left sides. The weight is taken on both hands at first, then on the right one only until the feet land to take the weight.

N.B. For flank and rear vaults performed, for example, to the right the spring from the board should be slightly to the left. This increases the amount of spring-up possible by the extended legs.

4. *Straddle*

This is a leapfrog movement in which the legs pass one either side of the horse in a wide position. The seat should not lift high as this causes the body to fall forward. Both hands are placed forward on the horse, after the spring. The legs extended straddle over the horse, while the head and trunk stay extended. The fingers need only to touch the horse, not grip. The legs are then brought smartly together for an extended landing. The hands from the horse come to the sides. It is a mistake to do this vault with the board close because the feeling of toppling forward will result, apart from the fact that it decreases flight. A slight relaxation is required in the feet and knees on landing. Once the straddling action is correct the gymnast can attempt to hollow a little before bringing the feet together. This makes for a perfectly executed landing.

Half-turn. The straddling action is made as before but very soon in the straddle the legs are brought together over the horse; to turn to the left, the left leg is brought to the right one and past it. This starts the turn which is helped by the hips and the head. The gymnast now faces the horse for landing. Again a slight hollow can be aimed for here, expecially as the impetus is backwards and the hollow out will bring the body weight over the feet and not beyond them. The hands may be used to balance on the horse at first until the turn is executed correctly and with confidence.

If these five vaults are introduced as part of a sequence it is possible that they will be performed satisfactorily from the start without the aid of a stand-by. For example, the suggestion may be made that a tucked position may be used to arrive on the horse and a tucked position off it; now, try to use a simple movement to get right over the horse. Similarly the suggestion can be made for putting the legs sideways over the apparatus. From this method the actual vaults may be coached, once they have been arrived at by the gymnast, by experimentation rather than 'This is a flank vault and everyone will do it'.

5. *Short-arm overthrow*

This is the first vault in which the gymnast is actually turning over completely, therefore it is wise to have a stand-by when first attempts are being made.

A little more flight is required for this vault than 1–4 because time must be given to get the feet above the head. If the board is close to the horse a piked short-arm position will result because the nearness of the horse makes the seat 'go over the top' to compensate. A short springy run is followed by flight from the board on to the hands. The arms are bent (strongly) but not relaxed, otherwise the chest will touch the horse. The head must be held back. The feet and legs pass extended through the handstand position, and the speed should be such that once the weight is over the hands it immediately lifts up and forwards so that the gymnast turns over to stand. The hands push away from the horse to give 'flight' off it. It takes a little time to learn to alight standing up, but with practice the current amount of push needed is felt to make the gymnast arrive on her feet. Too much extension of the arms too rapidly makes the gymnast fall forward on to her hands if the body weight is then travelling forwards.

It is hoped that most of these vaults will be executed with little or no help, but if help is needed then it should be given in different ways. *For the squat-over* stand to one side, near hand placed on the near wrist, far hand on the shoulder. *Straddle-over:* Stand in front and take both shoulders. Stand back as gymnast moves over the horse. It is possible to stand at the side, but care must be taken not to interfere with the gymnast's straddling leg. *Flank vault:* Stand at the side and take the arm over which the weight remains, i.e. the hand that stops on the horse landing opposite side from the feet. *Rear vault:* Stand on the side opposite to that over which the feet will pass. Legs to the right, stand on the left. It is possible to take only the arm which comes near to the stand-by, but assistance can be given on landing by standing behind the gymnast when she turns into the 'V' position. *Short arm:* Stand in at the side with near hand on wrist and far hand under the shoulder or under the small of the back, depending on the ability of the performer.

Vaults which require a spring from one foot

6. *Thief vault*

This vault demands a good space between the horse and the board because the free leg is swung up in front of the horse to clear it, joined by the other leg, then, when they have passed over the horse, the hands are placed on the horse to give a push. The arms should be straight, legs straight and as high a 'V' position as possible shown. The body should be hollowed to land. A very definite moment of time should be apparent when the body is poised over the horse before the hands touch. *To stand by:* Stand on the side and the rear arm once the hands are placed on the horse. The stand-by should be alert in case of the toes catching on the take-off. If this happens the gymnast may pitch forward, in which case the stand-by must use her ingenuity to manhandle to prevent an accident.

7. *Fencing rear vault*

A fencing movement is one which is taken from the side from one foot. In the rear vault the last foot to strike the board must be the one farthest from the horse. This allows space for the rear leg to lift, e.g. legs in rear vault to the left. Approach run sideways to the horse and place left foot on the board, right hand on the horse. Swing the right leg up, bearing weight on the supporting hand, as high as possible, then join the beating leg to it in 'V' position. The place of the right hand on the horse is taken by the left behind the back as the position passes over the horse. Finish facing to the side with the left hand on the horse.

Standing by: On the opposite side to the legs, i.e. near the head of the gymnast. Take the first arm with the rear hand and give a little support to the shoulder with the other hand. Dispense with standing by as soon as possible, expecially on vaults which do not demand turning upside down.

Some interesting work can be achieved by aiming at two or three specified movements but giving choice of apparatus. For example, tuck movements, straddle movements and 'V' sit positions. These can all be practised during agility work, developed on the beam, progressed on the bars and finally expressed as vaults. Similar movements have been taken, but the apparatus is so varied that differences appear at once. The apparatus also allows for the individual to experiment on her own but with a definite idea in mind.

8. *Layout movement*

This layout has been mentioned on bars and on the beam. Here it is used as a difficulty placed before the actual vault. Many of the simpler vaults can have their tariff raised by progressing the vault with a layout. A layout is a position in the air when the body is hollow and the legs pass above the horizontal. The layout must be performed quickly (the hollow) because it is followed by a quick pike at the hips. An example of this is a layout

41 Straight-leg drop back to catch the top bar. Thumb should *not* be round the bar

42 The drop-back movement on the rise to the bar

43 Straight-leg drop back to catch the top bar with a half-turn to the left

44 Hand position after the turn
(Bottom left)

45 Tremendous flight shown from the hands in the long arm vault
(Bottom right)

straddle. After the hands have been placed on the horse the spring is such that the feet and legs are thrown upwards and backwards, so that if a line were drawn on a wall level with the gymnast's head and parallel to the

FIG. 24

floor, then the feet must rise above it. Once above, the hips are flexed very sharply. This puts the hips high in the air to allow the legs to straddle round and over the horse to land.

A layout by a straight-leg squat brings the vaults into the high tariffs.

Tariff ten vaults

All vaults over the horse which pass through a straight-arm handstand position come under the ten tariff. These include long-arm overthrow, long arm, quarter-turn, long-arm quarter-turn and wheel-out, handstand squat and straddle and cartwheel. All of these positions have been used on either the bars or the beam from a static handstand position. Now it is necessary to execute these movements together with flight and speed. The timing for the squat vaults must be very exact, while the over-throw flight after the vault must be great to counteract

K

the speed. In every case the handstand must be shown (sideways in the cartwheel) with the arms at full stretch.

Approach run for these vaults. It is necessary to develop the run for these vaults to a high degree of perfection. Without this the vaults themselves will be of a poorer standard. As said before, speed and flight are necessary, therefore the run-up must not be guessed but worked out properly. This takes time and continual practice, because once the gymnast is tired the approach run ceases to be of value. The board may be placed on the floor, on its own, then a chalk mark made on the floor, preceding the board, to indicate where the last foot should be before alighting on the board. The gymnast should determine whether this is to be the right or the left foot. Once this step is made then it is a matter of practice to develop the run of twelve to sixteen steps, the last one to land on the chalk mark, then feet together on the board. The forward speed should be so great that it is not possible for the gymnast to spring from the board without rising high into the air. Because there is not a horse the coach may stand in front and, as the gymnast develops flight, take the weight of the body under the shoulders and move back. Gradually this can be perfected so that the coach supports under the hips, i.e. coach underneath. She must move back quickly, though, or the gymnast will go over her head.

A twelve-step run-up. The first few strides should be used to gather speed and the three or four simple coasting steps. This provides the control, but it does not mean that the speed is decreased. It is simply maintained but not increased further. A few little hesitant steps to start should be avoided, so should a hitch step, too, to get on to the right foot. The run should commence with the same foot, the twelve steps measured out, followed by the take-off from the board. Starting position should be noted by a chalk mark. Once all of these points are satisfactory then the gymnast can measure out her distance with her own feet (not a guess measure of a few running steps) or by the use of a piece of string stretched from the start to the board. When more than one gymnast is practising a measuring tape is of great value—each gymnast's run can then be marked on the tape. So far the approach has been from the start to the board. Now the flight distance must be noted and increased as improvement is made. The gymnast must use her run to the full and by doing this she will find that it is impossible to vault with the board very close. Gradually, the gap can be increased until a pleasing distance is found. This should be done in practice by moving the horse, not the board, once the run-up is fixed. In competition the board must be moved because the horse will be fixed to the floor.

Flight: This is the space of time from the feet leaving the board to the hands alighting on the horse. The flight must be high in order to alight on the horse with the arms extended. The feet should thrust away from the board upwards and backwards quickly. The greater the foot-thrust, the higher the flight. The higher the flight, the better the arm extension can be. This, in its turn, produces the speed for the second flight before landing.

FIG. 25

9. *Long-arm overthrow*

A fully extended position should be shown in handstand but the hands remain on the top of the horse for a moment only. The speed and flight carry the body through the position into a further flight where the body and legs should be parallel to the ceiling, the arms extended above the head. This extension should be maintained until the feet touch the floor, when a resilience in the feet and knees completes the overthrow. The trunk should be kept extended. In an overthrow the head plays an important part in keeping the handstand position, and also in the control of the landing, because the head is used as a brake together with the toes, which should grip the floor.

Fig. 26

10. *Handstand quarter-turn*

All the coaching for number 9 applies up to the flight into the handstand. From the handstand either the right or left hand is removed from the horse so that the body turns a quarter-turn to alight sideways to the horse. If the right hand is removed the weight is taken on to the left hand and the quarter-turn is made to the left. The body must remain hollow until the feet touch the floor. In the quarter-turn the head must be pressed back so that the pivoting occurs at the shoulders. In this vault there is much less second flight than in the long-arm overthrow. The quarter-turn can be practised from a kick up to handstand on the end of the box. Remove one hand and quarter-turn down. The quarter-turn can be assisted by standing on the side of the arm which is the weight-bearer, i.e. if the right hand bears the weight stand in on the right. The gymnast will land facing the coach.

FIG. 27

11. *Handstand quarter-turn and wheel-out*
In this vault the quarter-turn is made to replace the free hand on the horse so that the body faces sideways—e.g. handstand, move the right hand to quarter-turn to the left and replace it—side handstand. Wheel out from this position as in a cartwheel but with the legs together. The left hand leaves the horse first then the right hand with a push away to alight sideways, right side to the horse. The hollow position must be kept throughout until the landing is made. This vault can be practised, too, from the end of the box; also, if the gymnast has difficulty in doing the actual vault the coach can stand up on top of

the box and turn the body into the wheel-out position. If the right hand is being moved and replaced for the wheel, stand on the top of the box on the left. The position can actually be held with the gymnast's legs over the coach's shoulders.

12. *Handstand squat through* (*bent legs*)—quick beat off hands

The static handstand should be good before attempting the squat through the hands, so that when the flight and speed are added the actual vault is known. The flight up to the handstand remains the same. The handstand position must be felt, almost in a balance (or in a movement sequence go with speed and then stop). Once this position is achieved the shoulders are allowed to move forward over the hands and the legs are quickly bent to squat through the hands to alight facing forward on the mat. The head must be held back because this fixes the shoulder position to allow the body to lever on them. The handstand should not be cut short, otherwise the movement becomes a layout squat-through. The landing from a handstand squat, both bent and straight leg, is simple, once the cut-through feeling is achieved, because the gymnast does not overthrow, therefore the landing can be sighted the whole time.

13. *Handstand straight-leg squat*—quick beat off the hands

This is a very similar vault to number 12. From the handstand position the shoulders again are allowed to move forward on the hands, then fixed. The legs very quickly fold by piking sharply at the hips to pass the feet between the hands. The hands push away from the horse to turn the body upright again. This straight-leg squat is, in fact, easier than the bent-leg squat because there is the whip to be used when the legs are fully extended. This is lost in a bent-knee movement. The arms and legs must be kept at full extent, then, when the feet pass over the horse, the shoulders must be extended too. This produces, together with the hand push, a lift in the shoulders to allow the feet to clear. The landing is the same except that the legs are already stretched before landing. Head and trunk should remain erect.

14. *Handstand straddle down*—quick beat off hands
Once again this movement has been felt as a finish on the bars and beam, so that all that is required is to link the run-up with the movement. Once the handstand is reached, the hips pike strongly to fold the legs, the shoulders move forward and the head is kept back. The legs pass one either side of the horse. The straddle is completed by bringing the legs extended together before landing. The push from the hands through the shoulders rights the gymnast for landing feet first.

For the last three vaults the stand-by should take hold of the shoulder nearest to her by placing it in the cup of the hand. The other hand should be ready to stop the handstand from passing into an overthrow. Once this is prevented, both hands can be placed at the shoulders to allow the cut-through to occur. Care must be taken in the handstand straddle down to avoid catching the gymnast's legs. It is useful to be able to stand by in front, for this movement, with one hand on each shoulder, but should the gymnast not be able to stop the handstand the coach must quickly move to the side.

15. *Cartwheel*
This vault is a cartwheel only with the hands and the trunk. The legs remain together. It may be necessary to cut down the flight at first whilst timing the movement. Cartwheel on to the left hand. After the run and spring from the board, the body turns sideways, the left hand is placed on the horse, followed by the right hand. The

elbows should be extended and the head kept back. From
here the movement is the wheel-out as given in number 11,
except that it has a little more speed. The cartwheel passes
through sideways handstand with the body fully extended
to alight sideways to the horse with right side of the gymnast to the horse. To stand in for cartwheel and wheel-out
movements the coach must stand at the right side if the last
hand to leave the horse is the right, i.e. the weight-bearing
hand. The gymnast will land with her back to the coach.

TARIFF OF VAULTS

Thief vault	7
Flank vault	7
Straight-leg squat, bent body	7
Straddle half-turn	8
Layout above horizontal bent-leg squat	8·5
Flank and three-quarter-screw	8·5
Layout straight-leg squat	10
Layout and straddle	10
Handstand quarter-turn	10
Long-arm overthrow	10
Long-arm quarter-turn to wheel-out	10
Handstand straight-leg squat	10
Handstand straddle-down	10
Straddle up to handstand straight-leg squat-down	10
Sheep vault	10
Cartwheel	10

6

Code of Points for Gymnastics Competitions

Championships of the World and Olympic Games

1. All exercises voluntary and imposed are appreciated by five judges appointed by the Executive Committee. The judges hand in their written marks *independently*, then show them publicly. They all consult on the first and second exercises in order to find a standard mark. Of the five marks obtained the highest and the lowest are discarded and an aggregate taken of the other three.

The gap between the highest and the lowest of these must not be more than ·5 if the marks are above 8·5 and not more than 1 mark in every other case.

If the gap is too great then consultation must take place and if no decision can be reached then the jury will intervene.

Set exercises

2. Set exercises on floor, bars and beam are valued from 0 to 10 points by tenths of a point.

Five points are attributed to the rhythm and exactness of all parts of the exercise.

Five points for general impression, i.e. elegance and surety of the execution.

The vault will be valued:

Five points for technical value.

Five points for execution.

3. In order to allow a judge to be as precise as possible

the set work is divided into several parts, each having a value proportional to the difficulty. An established list of main faults and penalizations will be drawn up.

4. Except for floor exercises each gymnast may recommence without penalty any exercise which she considers to have done badly. She must disclose her intention to the jury before the judges make or show a mark. The recommencement must be done after a reasonable rest, but before the team leaves the piece of apparatus. The second attempt only is valuable. At the horse two attempts are allowed, the best mark to count.

5. All set work may be reversed but only in its entirety.

Voluntary exercises

6. Except for the vault these exercises may not be recommenced (continuation after a fall permitted).

7. Voluntary exercises are coded from 0 to 10 by tenths of a point divided in this way:

Five points, in which 2 are for execution and 3 for general impression.

8. Voluntary exercises must differ from set work and from one gymnast to another. Nevertheless, set movements may be incorporated into voluntaries provided that they are linked up differently.

9. All exercises of strength and force are considered undesirable. Preference should be given to movements with spirit. Movements must be executed in such a way as to avoid repetition and with original link-ups.

The entire exercise must have a technical value corresponding to the standard of the competition. Technique plus difficulty should be adapted to the physical make-up of each gymnast in order that the result may be easy and elegant.

10. Individual voluntary exercises must contain five elements of difficulty, of which *one* must be of the greatest difficulty. For each element less, the penalty is ·6 of a

mark. If no difficulty is introduced at all, then the loss of 3 full points should be envisaged.

11. (a) *Small faults ·1–·2*

    Poor head position.

    Toes not extended.

    Legs slightly flexed.

    Small stops which break the rhythm.

    Heavy, uncontrolled movements.

    Small steps or jumps on arrival on the floor.

(b) *Medium faults ·3–·5*

    Flexion or considerable bending of arms or legs.

    Flexion of the arms in reversed positions.

    Unintended flexion of the trunk.

    Touching the hands on the floor.

    Stiff movements instead of supple movements.

    Speaking to the gymnast by the coach.

    Poor interpretation of the text.

(c) *Grave faults ·5 and above*

    Help from the coach.

    Repetition of a would-be movement.

    Fall on the seat or knees.

    Falling in the course of a floor exercise.

    Movements added.

    Parts of the exercise omitted.

If the exercise is not finished marks should be given only for the part executed and the proportion, value and penalty taken into consideration.

Marks for general impression will be reduced in consequence.

Vault

12. All vaults must be performed by putting the hands on the horse. In both set and voluntary vaults the gymnast has two attempts. The last attempt to count. For voluntary vaults the two vaults may be different. The tariff of vaults

will be fixed by the Executive Committee. If the chosen
vault does not figure in the tariff then a written explana-
tion of it must be sent to the President of the Technical
Committee and a copy to the Secretary one month before
the competition. An extra attempt is allowed only if the
apparatus has not been touched. If the horse is touched,
then the vault is marked.

Vault penalties

Touching the horse with the feet	·5–2 marks
Flight insufficient	·5
Flight with bent body	·5
Leaving go with the hands too late	·5
Alighting from the horse badly directed or uncontrolled	Up to 2 marks
Omitting to hollow out before landing	Up to 2 marks
Help by the coach	Vault nullified

Landing

Landing hard and uncertain	·5
A step or jump	·2
Touching the floor with the hands	·5
Landing completely on the hands	1
Landing sitting or on the knees	1·5–2 marks
Landing awkwardly or falling against the horse	1
Help by the coach	1·5–2 marks

Vaults interrupted by sitting or putting the feet on the
horse—0 marks.

Each set vault executed not as it is written will be
marked—0 marks.

Assymetric bars

13. Movements of swinging and lightness must pre-
dominate; standing position (held) should be avoided.

Altogether avoid, on this apparatus, movements belonging to floor work and beam, e.g. held positions and bridge movements alone will be taken into consideration; real difficulty and all the finishes necessitate a manual grip.

Each fall incurs a deduction of 1 point provided that the gymnast remounts the equipment immediately. In the case of a three-second stop the exercise is considered finished.

Help by coach	1·5 marks
Assistance only on landing	·5

Beam

14. Beam exercises must be lively, must involve all parts of the body, must contain sitting, standing and lying positions, steps, jumps, turns and some held positions, but the latter must not dominate the exercise.

Execution should be continuous. Avoid monotony of the rhythm and maintain held positions. Finally, the exercise should be performed with fullness, surety, suppleness and elegance. Duration one minute thirty seconds to two minutes. The timekeepers must start their watches when the gymnast's feet leave the floor. For the set exercise as well as the voluntary the gymnast may recommence after a fall, but only from the place where the fall occurred, with a penalty of one mark. In the case of a fall of more than three seconds the exercise is considered finished. In the set work a new start is authorized from the beginning on condition that the gymnast has not touched the beam after the first attempt.

Added arm or leg movements for balance	3
Added trunk	Up to 1 mark
Held positions too short	·2–·4
Jumps too low and uncertain	·3
Walking in the place of running	·3
Falling	1 mark

Hanging or falling on the apparatus
   without putting the feet down   1 mark
Help from the coach   1·5
Help on landing   ·5

Floor Exercises

15. These exercises must be done using the entire body; containing some artistic jumps with plenty of vivacity, some positions, some symmetric and with expression. The space allowed is twelve metres and the gymnast should use all the floor area. The duration is one minute to one minute thirty seconds. The timekeepers commence timing when the gymnast moves her arms or legs. Both set and voluntary exercises must be performed with music. The character of the music should correspond with the presented exercise. During the exercise no help is authorized on the part of the coach. If the coach stands on the working area ·5 is deducted.

Gymnast out of working area:
    1 foot   ·1
    2 feet   ·2
    Faulty rhythm or unsuitable music   ·5

16. For the floor work and the beam a signal is given at the limit of the maximum time. Second signal after five seconds. If the exercise is not ended after the second signal ·5 is deducted; ·1 is deducted for every second under the required time.

DIMENSIONS FOR EQUIPMENT

Bars

High bar	230 cm from the floor
Low bar	150 cm
Length of the wooden bars	350 cm
Thickness of the oval bar	41 × 51 cm
Gap between the two bars	43 × 48 cm

Beam

Height of the beam	120 cm
Length	500 cm
Barrel shape—working surface	10 cm
Thickest part	13 cm
Depth of beam	16 cm

Board for take-off not more than 10 cm from the floor.

Horse

Length	160 cm
Width	35 cm
Height	110 cm

The horse must be fixed to the floor.

Board

Length	120 cm
Height at the front	12 cm

The board should be covered with a non-slip material.

Floor

A supple area of 14 metres × 14 metres covered by a carpet not less than 12 × 12 metres and with an underfelt of not less then 5–10 mm. The 12 metres should be clearly marked on the surface of the carpet, which should be non-slip.

Horse

Appendix

LADIES' FLOOR EXERCISES
BRITISH INDIVIDUAL 1962

Music: Chopin. Valse No. 10 in B Minor. Record: Columbia Ext. Play 7 in. SEL 1660 Side No. 2.

Commence at Bar No. 97. Take the two bars preceding as an introduction. Commence in centre floor, well to the front, and facing front. The count of 1, 2, 3, 4, 5, 6 equals two bars of music.

 1. To the R. diagonal make small lunge with *chassé* of R. foot bringing the arms from the sides, out to the side and softly forward to shoulder height palms downwards. (To the count of 1, 2, 3, 4, 5, 6.) L. foot pointed on the toe.

 2. Three open turns to the L. back diagonal. L.R.L. arms opening to the side. (Count 1, 2, 3, 4, 5, 6.)

 3. Cartwheel on R. leg. Cartwheel on L. leg, still travelling in the left diagonal. (Count 1, 2, 3, 4, 5, 6 for each Cartwheel.)

 4. Step on R. foot behind L. foot, step to the side with L. foot, step forward and hop on R. foot stretching L. leg lifted behind arms moving softly out to sides on the steps and moving downwards to stretch forward to shoulder height palms upwards on the hop. (Count 1, 2, 3, 4, 5, 6.)

 5. Step behind with lifted L. leg making a quarter L. turn, weight on L. foot, stretch R. foot and point on the toe. R. arm lifted to high oblique, L. arm stretched forward at shoulder height. (Count 1, 2, 3, 4, 5, 6.) (Show a good hollow pos. of back.)

 6. Forward walkover on R. foot bending R. leg, R. toe on L. knee, whilst in the air, landing on L. foot. (Count 1, 2, 3, 4, 5, 6.)

 7. Three running steps forward, with waltz rhythm, and gallop step, knees high with good elevation (Count 1, 2, 3, 4,

5, 6), arms out to sides on runs and to the back on gallop, with a forward bend of the body.

8. *Chassé* step on the R. foot, close L. foot to R. Step R. foot and swing L. leg forward with a quarter R. turn, look at the leg with arms out to sides and immediately make half R. turn, R. arm lifted forward and upward, L. arm back in line with lifted L. leg (*fouetté*). (Count 1, 2, 3, 4, 5, 6.)

9. Lunge back on L. foot, backward bend of the body, take the arms sideways and backwards over the head. (Count 1, 2, 3, 4, 5, 6.)

10. Handstand into forward roll. (Count 1, 2, 3, 4, 5, 6.)

11. Immediately, and before standing fully, pick up the left instep in the L. hand, and lift the leg high and bend behind, take the body forward, with the R. hand and arm reaching towards the ground, oblique with palm facing floor. (Count 1, 2, 3, 4, 5, 6.)

12. Relax to deep squat, knees forward, L. foot behind R. foot. L. arm downward, forward and oblique, R. arm downward, backward and oblique. (Count 1, 2, 3, 4, 5, 6.) Stretch up to stand, using a pushing movement of the palms upwards to full stretch with a R. twist of the body, L. arm forward, oblique and upward; R. arm backward, oblique and upward, finishing still on the toes and head thrown back. (Count 1, 2, 3, 4, 5, 6.)

13. Run and handspring. (Count 1, 2, 3, 4, 5, 6./1, 2, 3, 4, 5, 6.) Stretch up arms over head.

14. Small lunge forward, R. foot with lilt, arms softly forward and crossing in front to open out sideways and backwards, then back walkover to land on R. foot. (Count 1, 2, 3, 4, 5, 6./1, 2, 3, 4, 5, 6.)

15. L. foot to slide backwards into splits position, both arms sideways. (Count 1, 2, 3, 4, 5, 6.)

Move R. arm to sweep forward over R. foot, continue round in a full circle in front of body to sideways stretch. (Count 1, 2, 3, 4, 5, 6.)

16. Left circle of R. leg over the top of L. leg. R. hand supporting body on the ground, a full L. turn of the body, to kneel on R. knee and sit back on left heel, arms in ring position over head, hollow back. Continue with half L. turn of body, rise

up on knee and turn on it, L. leg stretched forward, take the
R. arm down to L. foot and the L. arm backwards. Take the
weight forward on to the L. foot, bend the L. knee to stand
and make a 120-degree L. turn, take the L. arm downwards
and upwards to stretch; R. arm upwards and backwards and to
low oblique, in line with R. leg which is stretched backwards on
the toe, head looking towards back foot. (Movements between
the marked stars to be continuous and to the count of 1, 2, 3,
4, 5, 6./1, 2, 3, 4, 5, 6.)

17. (*Coupé, chassé, pas de bourrée* starting on L. foot, and
repeat on R. performed with lightness and travelling forward
diagonally.)

The definition of *coupé, chassé, pas de bourrée* is as follows:

The R. foot is pointed behind and it is brought forward to
cut away the L. foot, the weight then being on the R. foot;
immediately slide the L. foot into a slight lunge position, take
the weight on the L. foot, step behind with R. foot forward
diagonal with L. and step in front with R. The three steps are
performed on the toes with a turned-out position of the feet
and knees. (1, 2, 3, 4, 5, 6./1, 2, 3, 4, 5, 6.)

18. Finish last movement with L. foot crossed in front of R.
Step into the R. diagonal on R. and L. making a full turn with
R. foot resting on and in front of the R. shin. Step again and
repeat pirouettes. (1, 2, 3, 4, 5, 6.)

19. Step forward on to R. foot into arabesque balance
both hands reaching forward and downwards. (1, 2, 3, 4, 5, 6.)

20. *Pas de basque* on L. foot turning to the L. and *pas de
basque* on R. foot still turning L. (1, 2, 3, 4, 5, 6.) Arms softly
from L. to R.

21. Three running steps L.R.L., split-leap with R. leg in
front, *chassé* backwards on L. foot and hop lifting R. knee up
to chin, arms diagonally backwards and downwards. (1, 2, 3,
4, 5, 6./1, 2, 3, 4, 5, 6.)

22. Step into R. diagonal with R. foot, join the L. to the R.
and step R. swinging the L. leg high, make a half-turn replacing the L. leg with the R. (*chassé, grand jetté* turning 1, 2, 3, 4, 5,
6), arms lifting high over the head, body arched on the turn.

23. Three runs R.L.R., scissor kick (1, 2, 3, 4, 5, 6), arms
out to sides. Three runs forward R.L. gallop step making full

turn in air, step R. foot, step L. foot and spin to L., full turn in slight curl position with R. foot at the side of L. knee; R. leg bent (1, 2, 3, 4, 5, 6./1, 2, 3, 4, 5, 6), arms softly crossed in front of body.

24. Lilt forward on to R. foot stretching arms forward palms upwards. (1, 2, 3, 4, 5, 6.)

25. Step back on L. foot, step back on R. foot, L. foot pointed forward, arms circling downwards and backwards; R. arm in high oblique, L. in forward horizontal. (1, 2, 3, 4, 5, 6.)

26. Half cartwheel on L. hand to forward roll bending L. leg on roll to stand on R. leg, L. leg stretched behind. (1, 2, 3, 4, 5, 6./1, 2, 3, 4, 5, 6.) Both arms lifted.

27. Join feet together and a high dive followed by forward roll. (1, 2, 3, 4, 5, 6.)

28. Step to the left with L. foot, point R. foot to the side, bend sideways, L. arm lifted over head and R. arm softly in front of body. (1, 2, 3, 4, 5, 6.) Step to the right, bend sideways with L. foot resting on the back calf of R. leg, R. arm lifted over head, L. arm softly in front of body. (1, 2, 3, 4, 5, 6.)

29. Spin to the left one and three-quarter times, starting in low curled position, rising to stretched position on toes, arms over head. (1, 2, 3, 4, 5, 6./1, 2, 3, 4, 5, 6.)

30. Run forward, tinska (on either hand), finish with one foot pointed behind opposite arm raised forward and upward, other arm stretched behind.

Come to attention when music has finished.

NORTH EASTERN AMATEUR GYMNASTIC ASSOCIATION

Junior and Senior Ladies' Set Work for the 1960 Championships.

Floor Exercises

1. Standing, feet astride, leaning to the left, weight on L. foot—both arms sideways to the left.

2. Transfer weight to R. foot and with full turn of 360 degrees place L. foot forward on ground, arms sideways.

3. Hop on L. foot, L. arm high oblique forward, R. arm low oblique backward.

4. Step on to R. foot sideways, circle left arm down and across body and throw in cartwheel on the L. hand—finish feet astride, arms sideways.

5. Body bending quarter-turn to left bending R. leg (*plié*). R. arm circle over top to reach towards L. foot. L. arm high oblique backward.

6. Lower L. arm and bring forward to the right in front.

7. Lift both arms up through ring above head and lower arms sideways, body quarter-turn right.

8. One *chassé* step *grand jetté* to the left, finish with feet astride, weight on L. foot, arms sideways.

9. Place both arms to the left sideways and spin one-and-a-quarter-turn (450 degrees), to the right and step on L. foot.

10. Arabesque balance—L. arm forward low, R. arm following line of L. leg. Hold for 3 seconds.

11. Bring R. foot to the left, slight supple bend of trunk, arms circling in opposite directions; R. foot forward to side, L. foot backward to side.

12. Triple runs beginning with R. foot (R.L.R.) (L.R.L.). Step on R. foot and *fouetté* turn throwing L. foot forward. Step on L. and lift R. leg bent in front, L. arm rounded in front at shoulder height, R. arm rounded above head. Show position.

13. Step on R. foot then L. foot lowering arms sideways and throw for handstand forward roll.

14. Stand up, both feet together, and place L. foot forward on point, weight on R. foot. With arms to right, circle L. leg round 360 degrees, placing it to kneel on the floor. Slide R. leg straight and lift arms to ring above head.

15. Lower arms sideways across body and open sideways while bending R. leg to stand.

16. Rise on toes. With a few steps run and handspring. Stand up.

HIGH AND LOW BAR SET ROUTINE

1. Stand facing low bar.
2. Long swing underneath low bar and squat both feet between hands to sit on low bar, legs straight. Immediately transfer hands to high bar and circle both legs over high bar to front-leaning rest on high bar.
3. Swing legs forward and backward and straddle legs over high bar around hands. (Hold 2 seconds.)
4. Drop backwards to half-inverted hang, legs still in straddle position.
5. Bring legs together, shoot both legs forward, at the same time releasing R. hand and with half-left turn of body grasp high bar with R. hand in forward grasp.
6. On forward swing of body circle the bottom bar to front-leaning rest.
7. Swing legs forwards and backwards and squat straight legs through hands to back-leaning rest. Transfer both hands to high bar.
8. Cut R. leg under L. leg, stretch both legs forward and bounce from bottom bar over high bar, legs together, to front-leaning rest.
9. Place both hands on bottom bar and throw to handstand, bend R. knee and place R. knee on high bar. (Hold for 2 seconds.)
10. Stretch R. leg, bringing R. leg to L. leg into handstand position and squat both legs through hands to ground.

LADIES' HIGH AND LOW BAR SET

Stand one pace back from high bar facing low bar. With a spring jump to catch low bar and long under swing, on backward swing place R. leg between hands to finish upright astride low bar. Immediately half L. turn and backward mill circle, lift R. leg over low bar and replace R. hand outside R. leg, throw to hock swing to catch high bar with reverse grasp. Releasing R. hand, half R. turn to face low bar and replace R. hand on high bar (both hands in ordinary grasp). Lift straight R. leg to the R. and over low bar. Lift straigh L. leg to the L. over low bar and place foot on low bar. With a kick pull over high bar to front rest. Jump R. leg between hands and lift L. leg to the L. over high bar to sitting position, replacing L. hand on outside of L. leg. Drop back keeping legs straight and with a beat, cut legs out under R. hand replacing R. hand on high bar. Swing legs down and up to the left and place R. leg over low bar.

Place R. hand on low bar in front of body, swing L. leg down and backwards to the left and lift over low bar placing L. hand on low bar (front rest facing high bar). Swing legs under low bar and on backward swing squat on to low bar. Grasp high bar, straighten legs and immediately straddle over high bar with a half L. or R. turn to alight standing facing high bar.

JUNIOR BEAM SET, 1961

1. Stand facing the centre of the beam. With a run place both hands on the beam and squat over to sit in riding seat, Lift L. leg over beam.

2. Bring legs together and V-sit with hands behind on beam. Drop R. foot on to beam and stand placing L. foot forward with weight on it. R. foot on beam. Arms reach forward to stand, then lower and raise sideways into ring position above head but with R. shoulder back, and left forward. (Wave movement through body when standing.)

3. Lower arms sideways. Two steps forward R.L. Swing R. leg forward and back then half-turn to R. finishing with weight on the L. foot, R. leg bent, knee high. Arms swing forward and backwards to finish with L. arm parallel to beam, shoulder height and R. arm above head, arm straight and head well back.

4. Pause. Circle R. arm backwards and up to join the L. arm parallel to beam. Step on R. foot and comat step twice (L.R.L.R.). Arms from forward position drop to sides and circle

forwards with each comat step then swing forward. (Comat step is like a gallop step.)

5. Step forward L. then R. with half-turn to right on R. foot into arabesque with L. leg raised behind. Arms swing back to oblique position backwards. Standing leg straight (balance is obliquely across beam). Hold for 2 secs.

6. Swing L. leg down and forward then turn three-eighths to right keeping L. leg off the beam behind. Arms pass through ring above head on turn. To finish, L. arm back, R. arm forward on shoulder level, L. shoulder back.

7. Step on to L. foot, two spring hops, R. in front of left, L. in front of right then two feather steps—step on R. foot and immediately sit on beam, L. leg in front. Arms sideways softly all the time lowering and rising with the energy of the springs.

8. Place both legs together and back-roll with head off beam on to R. knee, L. leg held high and head back.

9. Lower L. leg and place foot on beam, forward to stand, arms sideways. Small preparation with arms for spin, half-turn to right (back spin) to place R. foot beside the L.

10. Raise arms forward and spring into forward roll and squat up to stand, R. foot in front of left. Step forward on to L. foot, arms prepare to the L. Swing R. leg across L. for momentum then half-turn to the R. to face opposite way, (while the body turns only 180 degrees the R. leg completes a full circle). Arms finish obliquely back and low, palms turned out, body arched.

11. Spring on to R. foot, L. foot behind R. and spring, change feet to finish, L. in front. Arms—R. arm forward, L. back, when R. foot is front and vice versa.

12. Step on to R. foot and then L., circle arms backwards overhead then forwards and place hands on the beam. Kick to handstand and change legs in the air to land on R. leg. Stand up, arms from above head lower sideways.

13. Step on to L. foot and leap to the R. Step on L. then R. and kick to handstand and at once move R. hand along beam, wheel out. Finish R. side to the beam.